A Naturalist
and Other Beasts

Books by George B. Schaller

The Mountain Gorilla
The Year of the Gorilla
The Deer and the Tiger: A Study of Wildlife in India
The Tiger: Its Life in the Wild (with M. Selsam, for children)
The Serengeti Lion
Serengeti: A Kingdom of Predators
Golden Shadows, Flying Hooves
Mountain Monarchs: Wild Sheep and Goats of the Himalaya
Wonders of Lions (with K. Schaller, for children)
Stones of Silence: Journeys in the Himalaya
The Giant Pandas of Wolong (with J. Hu, W. Pan, and J. Zhu)
Gorilla: Struggle for Survival in the Virungas (with M. Nichols)
The Last Panda
Tibet's Hidden Wilderness
Wildlife of the Tibetan Steppe
Antelopes, Deer, and Relatives (edited with E. Vrba)

A Naturalist
and Other Beasts

TALES FROM A LIFE IN THE FIELD

George B. Schaller
with photographs by the author

SIERRA CLUB BOOKS

San Francisco

Copyright © 2007 by George B. Schaller

Portions of this book have appeared previously in other publications; see page 271 for full acknowledgment of copyrighted material.

Published by Sierra Club Books
85 Second Street, San Francisco, CA 94105
www.sierraclub.org/books

Produced and distributed by
University of California Press
Berkeley and Los Angeles, California
University of California Press, Ltd.
London, England
www.ucpress.edu

SIERRA CLUB, SIERRA CLUB BOOKS, and the Sierra Club design logos are registered trademarks of the Sierra Club.

Library of Congress Cataloging-in-Publication Data

Schaller, George B.
   A naturalist and other beasts : tales from a life in the field / George B. Schaller ; with photographs by the author
      p. cm.
   Includes bibliographical references (p.   ).
   ISBN-13: 978-1-57805-129-8 (alk. paper)
   ISBN-10: 1-57805-129-0 (alk. paper)
      1. Zoology--Field work--Anecdotes. 2. Animals--Anecdotes. 3. Schaller, George
B.--Travel. I. Title.

QL51.S387 2007
590--dc22   2006051153

Book and jacket design by Elizabeth Watson

Printed in the United States of America on acid-free paper.

11 10 09 08 07
10 9 8 7 6 5 4 3 2 1

Photo on preceding page: The author in 1991 on one of his many journeys in the Chang Tang region of northern Tibet to study and work on behalf of its wildlife. PHOTO BY KAY SCHALLER.

To my sons,

Eric and Mark, in fond remembrance

of shared field trips

Contents

THE HIMALAYA AND
THE TIBETAN PLATEAU

Acknowledgments

I would like to express my deepest gratitude collectively to the various countries that hosted me over the years, and to the many local organizations, scientists, officials, villagers, nomads, and others who collaborated with me, assisted in the field, and offered hospitality. The Wildlife Conservation Society sponsored many of the conservation efforts described here; in addition, the generous support of the National Geographic Society, National Science Foundation, Liz Claiborne–Art Ortenberg Foundation, Sacharuna Foundation, Armand Erpf Fund, and other donors made the work possible. I also thank Sierra Club Books editor Diana Landau for her dedicated efforts in assembling and editing the manuscript.

He who would do good to another must do it in Minute Particulars. General Good is the plea of the scoundrel, hypocrite, and flatterer; For Art and Science cannot exist but in minutely organized Particulars.

—William Blake, *Jerusalem,* chapter 3

In the relations of man with animals, with the flowers, with the objects of creation, there is a great ethic, scarcely perceived as yet, which will at length break forth into light.

—Victor Hugo

If thy heart be right, then will every creature be to thee a mirror of life, and a book of holy doctrine.

—Thomas à Kempis, 1427

Introduction

Of Marvels and Memories

It has been said that when naturalists retire, they write forewords and publish retrospectives. In presenting this anthology, I am not in search of memories: my interests lie in the future. Indeed, I wrote a draft of this introduction in the mountains of northern Afghanistan, where I was censusing Marco Polo sheep and promoting conservation. Since 1952 I have roamed through many countries, finding pleasure in observing animals and striving to protect them from the relentless attrition that affects all wild lands. I live in a geography of dreams, in a sense, always searching in my imagination for places where I might help to conserve the diversity of life for the benefit of all beings—including the local people whose future also depends on a healthy environment. As a Chinese proverb states, "All the flowers of all tomorrows are in the seeds of today."

Because of fortuitous circumstances, I have been associated with the Wildlife Conservation Society (once known as the New York Zoological Society) for more than half a century. The society has promoted the protection of wildlife since 1895. Its vision has served as my ideal, and this has enabled me to make fieldwork and conservation my life, becoming a wanderer of wastelands, mountains, and forests. The poet Walt Whitman asked, "But where is what I started for so long ago? And why is it yet unfound?" There is no final destination in conservation. Imbued with a moral obligation to fight on behalf of nature's beauty and integrity, to leave timeless mementos of wilderness, I have chosen a never-ending path—but one where I can make a difference. So today, at over seventy years old, I still strive to protect something that will outlive me, some small achievement that matters, whether it concerns the last Asiatic cheetahs in Iran or the great migrations of gazelles on Mongolia's eastern steppes.

After traversing North America in 1840, John C. Fremont wrote that "it was all wild and unexplored, and the uninvaded silence roused curiosity and invited research." My spirit resides in such places. Fortunately, important remnants of wildness persist. One is the plains and woodlands of Tanzania's Serengeti, where my wife, Kay, our two small sons, and I spent more than three years, perhaps the happiest of our lives. Another is the vast and wondrous upland of Tibet's Chang Tang, with its Tibetan antelope (chiru), wild asses and yaks, and other wildlife, a place to which I have devoted two decades.

My passion and profession have taken me to many lands as a sympathetic trespasser and roving researcher cooperating with local scientists, officials, and governments, gathering the detailed knowledge upon which conservation must be based, so that I can promote and prod to preserve fragments of a country's natural heritage. I learned long ago that conservation has no victories, that one must retain connections and remain involved with animals and places that have captured the heart—mountain gorillas, the Arctic National Wildlife Refuge—to prevent their destruction. I am sometimes asked why, given a world that is ever more wounded and scarred, I do not simply give up, burdened by pessimism. But conservation is my life: I must retain hope.

This anthology is primarily about animals, however, rather than the complexities of conservation. My greatest pleasure is to record an animal's daily life through quiet observation or even just by examining tracks, feeding sites, and other artifacts of its passing. I enjoy writing about what I saw in my quest to unveil the intricacies of another species, to author its biography. I have no access to the thoughts and desires of a capybara, of course, but I can at least describe the richness of its life, my methodical science leavened a little by intuition and feeling.

Zhen-Zhen, the female giant panda who was one of our study animals, rests among umbrella bamboo in China's Wolong Nature Reserve.

From dozens of published articles or accounts in books I have assembled nineteen stories from different parts of the world, mainly about animals I studied or that aroused my curiosity, and in a few cases about whole habitats. Because the pieces span half a century of field-work, certain specific information may be out of date. (The original date of publication is given at the end in each case.) My introductions to each chapter provide some current information, and where it seemed essential the original text has been minimally edited or annotated.

The ordering of chapters shows, I think, that while my emphasis on natural history remains constant, my career has subtly changed. No longer do I spend years studying a species. Instead I seek neglected countries where I might make a difference in conservation—most recently in Iran, Tajikistan, and Afghanistan. My mission has broadened to preserving ecosystems, including concern for the human cultures that affect them.

A number of my studies are based on scientific questions that intrigued me—some important, others trivial. What impact does lion predation have on prey populations? Are blue sheep related more closely to sheep or goats, based on their behavior? But I would not be truthful in suggesting that I always begin projects with logical reasons and plans. After all, such abstraction is new in our human evolution, whereas emotions are old, part of our ancient brain. A strong feeling of wanting to be in the Himalaya first drew me there; only then did studying the snow leopard become a goal. The powerful elegance of a tiger and the visual appeal of a giant panda evoke deep emotions, which enable us to form a bond with another species and lead to a desire for deeper understanding, one beyond soulless statistics. I cannot be a detached observer. I need to feel commitment to an animal or a place in order to devote years to it, often under harsh conditions. Not all the subjects of these writings evoke this response: occasionally I meet animals, such as the takin, with whose lives I have only a passing acquaintance but which provide delightful moments worth sharing.

I was fortunate to have been part of the golden age of wildlife studies, from the 1950s to the end of the twentieth century, when many large mammals—even such familiar and spectacular ones as the elephant and jaguar—for the first time became the focus of intensive research. And I was equally fortunate in having mentors who encouraged me and offered opportunities. Among these were Brina Kessel at the University of Alaska; John Emlen at the University of Wisconsin; Olaus and Mardy Murie, whom I joined in 1956 on a wildlife survey of the Alaska region that became the Arctic National Wildlife Refuge; and William Conway of the Wildlife Conservation Society. My interests had already been defined as a youngster, but such mentors guided me into becoming a scientific explorer of nature and, just as important, into embracing the spiritual values of wildlife and wilderness. The other indispensable partner has been Kay, who assisted with fieldwork on so many projects from the Congo to China, shared satisfaction and sacrifice, and made transitory homes for us in huts and tents.

Patiently observing animals may seem an antiquated pleasure in this age of computer modeling and remote sensing. I started as a pioneer and sometimes have felt left in the past as the focus of natural science has shifted. Universities neglect courses in natural history, yet such knowledge is the cornerstone of conservation. It provides basic information, defines problems, and suggests realistic solutions. Even the rhetoric of conservation has changed. Nature has now become "natural resources," viewed all too often only in economic terms and treated as a commodity to be sold, bought, or discarded. Appreciation of beauty, a sense of wonder, and the ethics of taking responsibility for other species and the land seldom enter official conservation discourse now. But I remain convinced that an appeal for conservation must reach the heart, not just the mind. Intimate portraits of animals help to inspire concern for their tenuous future, create a feeling of kinship, and convey that they too have a right to exist. Conservation without moral values cannot sustain itself.

The careless rapture of my early studies has been replaced more and more by efforts to protect animals and their habitats, using any argument and initiative that may have impact both locally and internationally: scientific, political, economic, aesthetic, ethical, religious. This has taken my time away from the satisfying occupation of natural history fieldwork. So, contrary to what I said at the beginning of this essay, perhaps I am creating this book to reclaim memories, reading over my work with nostalgia, reliving precious months and years.

For now, the animals and their homes described here endure. But the battles on their behalf continue. These writings are, in effect, a record of marvels and a sharing of memories. I hope that they give readers an enjoyable connection to creatures and places worth protecting for many reasons, not least because they are beautiful.

Prologue

Feral Biologist

The Scientist does not study nature because it is useful to do so. He studies it because he takes pleasure in it; and he takes pleasure in it because it is beautiful. If nature were not beautiful, it would not be worth knowing and life would not be worth living. . . . I mean the intimate beauty which comes from the harmonious order of its parts and which a pure intelligence can grasp.

—French mathematician Jules Poincaré (1854–1912)

When *Wildlife Conservation* magazine asked me to offer insights as to why a field biologist is a field biologist, I easily contained my enthusiasm. After all, the reasons for any quest dwell deep within us and are not always accessible even to introspection. Also, it's not difficult to find moral justification for what one likes to do. What has priority: possible benefits to science and conservation, or a self-indulgent life outdoors? When searching for a personal philosophy to vindicate one's taste, one might do well to recall the words of the German poet Johann Friedrich von Schiller, who wrote: "What the inner voice says will not disappoint the hoping soul."

How do you define a field biologist? Presumably he or she is not merely a person who views a trip to the wilderness as a refreshing interval, a touch of scientific ecotourism. One test of authenticity might be the length of time this biologist lives afield: someone who suffers from culture shock not when settling into a project but on returning home. "Feral biologist," as an article once called me, is a more apt description than field biologist.

However, random thoughts on field biology may be useful if for no reason other than to dispel the notion, fostered by television, that we biologists usually lead romantic and adventurous lives. Even seemingly easy projects such as studying lethargic lions and amiable apes require long days and nights without sleep, tracking animals through dank or thorny vegetation. Some species are solitary, shy, nocturnal, and reluctant to be observed. Searing heat and arctic cold are the field biologist's frequent companions. Tropical diseases are an occupational hazard, and political upheavals are annoying distractions. Cut off from urban amenities, a perpetual emigrant isolated in alien cultures, affected by an unsettled family life, a field biologist must work for years toward an elusive goal that local coworkers are often reluctant to embrace and perhaps unable to comprehend. A spouse must share these hardships as well as endure long separations. And it's not always easy to tolerate another's obsession.

Most research is mundane, a tedious and repetitive process of recording facts. Patience becomes a more valuable commodity than intellect. One must be resigned to waiting: waiting for the animal to appear, for the rain or the snow to stop, for the porters to arrive. Then there is the pressure to do well; for whatever the problems that confront you, you want to justify the financial support others have given your project, and you are in a competition—with yourself, as well as with all previously established standards of excellence. Adventures are rare and, at any rate, usually result from bad luck, poor planning, or carelessness. Indeed, a field biologist's greatest danger lies not in encounters with fierce creatures and treacherous terrain, but in being seduced by the comforts of civilization.

The naturalist William Beebe noted, "After we have tried to be sandpipers and ants, silversides and mackerel, we may attain to the honor of

This white-lipped peccary was a pet during my time studying jaguars in the Pantanal swamps of Brazil, 1977. PHOTO BY KAY SCHALLER.

such knowledge as our prejudiced, but humbled minds will permit." But these days anxiety and guilt about the fate of the animals we are studying cast shadows on our research. Curiosity is tinged with sympathy, a premonition that we are witness to the last days of Eden.

Where, then, lies the attraction of fieldwork? Are field biologists weird people given to scientific masochism? I can speak only for myself.

As a boy, I collected birds' eggs; kept a mini-zoo of salamanders, snakes, opossums, and other creatures; and liked to roam the countryside. Later, during my undergraduate years at the University of Alaska—which I chose partly for its wilderness setting—I discovered that I could extend boyhood activities into a legitimate adult pastime. Curiosity about the natural world is inherent, I suspect, in a field biologist. I am referring not to the abstract intellectual curiosity of a laboratory biologist who uses animals as tools to elucidate some concept, but to an emotional involvement that treasures animals for themselves,

In 1991, Kay and I revisited the Virunga Volcanoes, where we had lived while studying mountain gorillas in 1959 and 1960. Here we are on the summit of Mount Visoke.

enriching us by a sense of kinship. To me fieldwork is not a career but the core of my existence.

A project has its genesis in a scientific question that is worth answering, a valid goal that is worth fulfilling. Good research also demands a passion to understand, emotional commitment, and an urge to probe beyond the limits of knowledge. In the 1950s, when I began fieldwork, a one-year study of a species was generally considered ample. Now a study ideally involves at least the normal life span of an animal, perhaps fifteen years for lions and fifty years for elephants. Yet, no matter how deeply I immerse myself in another species, after three years or so my mind grows restless and seeks new goals, striving to break new ground. I can rationalize this by saying that other creatures perceive the world in ways so unimaginably different from us that I can record only the most basic facts about them. But I may simply have a short attention span. Although my research reports are limited, I find it deeply satisfying to provide a species, for the first time, with a new reality, a written history, especially if I also am able to convey the joy of discovery, the pleasure of a new insight.

I look for aesthetic experiences with animals, as well as intellectual involvement. Some of the species I have studied—mountain gorilla, tiger, giant panda—have such a transcendent beauty that it becomes an almost sensual pleasure to be near them. Through photographs and words an objective vision fuses with subjective feeling. Though photographs are often little more than sentimental evocations, idealized scenes that appeal to a sense of beauty and arouse compassion, at their best they create a harmony that encompasses both viewer and subject, forging a bond between us and the snow leopard or the butterfly in ways that words alone cannot achieve. Pen and camera are potent weapons against oblivion, helping species to survive—or serving as memorials.

Another idiosyncrasy determines what and where I study: I like to explore the physical as well as the intellectual realm. The more rare and remote a species, the greater the challenge to become the chronicler of its life. I view myself basically as a nineteenth-century wanderer with a scientific bent on an intangible and elusive search. There is an atavistic pleasure in crossing the Tibetan Plateau, our camel caravan lonely and lost between earth and sky, or trailing a string of porters through the mysterious silence of a rainforest. At times I have been labeled misanthropic because I usually avoid the conviviality of a scientific team on such ventures. Aside from my wife, Kay, and my sons, I prefer my own kind in small doses.

Author Peter Fleming noted some years ago that "the trouble about journeys nowadays is that they are easy to make but difficult to justify." Conservation now offers ample justification. I began to study animals out of curiosity. But anyone who observes the exponential destruction of wilderness must become an advocate for conservation. To preserve a remnant of beauty becomes an ideal, and this ideal possesses one until it is transformed into a faith. I was fortunate that my earliest fieldwork instilled in me an awareness of the need to leaven science with thought about the survival of species. In 1956, for example, I accompanied Olaus and Margaret Murie on a biological survey of America's last great wilderness, an area that would, through their efforts, soon become the Arctic National Wildlife Refuge. (See Chapter 1.) Over the years I have evolved from biologist to conservation biologist: research enhances my role as an ecological missionary. The goal is to balance knowledge and action.

Conservation problems are social and economic, not scientific, yet biologists have traditionally been expected to solve them. Research is easy; conservation most decidedly is not. Since conservation cannot be imposed from above, it must ultimately be based on local interests, skills, and traditions. A field biologist must work with local people and institutions to find innovative solutions. The establishment of a nature reserve often creates hostility, for, deprived of their land, local people are no longer able to collect fuel, hunt, and graze livestock. The traditional lives of indigenous people must be considered. Unfortunately, appeals to moral enlightenment seldom lead to progress; one cannot discuss the philosophy of conservation with a man cutting the last tree for fuel. Principles must always be juggled with practicalities. Seldom clear-cut, environmental issues often involve moral ambiguity. Instead of being just a biologist, something for which I was trained, I must also be an educator, diplomat, fundraiser, politician, anthropologist. . . . No wonder that I seek solitude; physical obstacles are minor compared to political ones.

Environmental destruction will never cease, not even in a truly moral world. Sustainable development, the Holy Grail of today's conservation movement, will not save that which many treasure most: pieces of wilderness undeveloped, unaffected by greed, where we can experience the calm rhythm of life and recapture a feeling of belonging to the natural world. Wilderness is a state of mind, and though it is a part of our past, it is doubtful that future generations will even miss it. They may grow apart from the wild. But they should be given the option of glimpsing the splendor that once was. We all strive for a private sense of merit; in addition, I now aspire to an ideal beyond science, in that my goal is to help fragments of wilderness endure.

[1992]

THE AMERICAS

What is life? It is the flash of a firefly in the night. It is the breath of a buffalo in the winter time. It is the little shadow which runs across the grass and loses itself in the sunset.

—Crowfoot, a Blackfoot Indian, 1890

And that's why I have to go back
to so many places in the future,
there to find myself
with no witness but the moon
and then whistle with joy,
ambling over rocks and clods of earth,
with no task but to live,
with no family but the road.

—Pablo Neruda, "End of the World"

Arctic Legacy

Caribou

This article on the Arctic National Wildlife Refuge in Alaska was published in 1990, during the presidency of George Bush the Elder, who had made oil drilling on the caribou calving grounds in the refuge a cornerstone of his energy policy—rather than improving fuel efficiency of vehicles or other alternatives. Naturally I was outraged at even the thought of such ecological vandalism, especially because some three decades earlier I had spent a marvelous summer with caribou in what later became the Arctic Refuge. In 1957, a year after my visit, I wrote to Secretary of the Interior Fred Seaton, urging him to give full protection to the refuge, without which it "may well in future years resemble one of the former Texas oil fields."

In writing thus, I certainly had no prescience that half a century later this trench war between commerce and conservation would again rage. President Bill Clinton opposed the destruction of America's last great wilderness and gave the refuge a reprieve. But with the ascendancy of Bush the Younger, the assault on the refuge became intense, as our country's natural heritage was subverted by a political process based not on a coherent energy policy but on greed, party politics, and an apparent indifference to the future. In recent years Congress has tried to attach drilling provisions to the Railroad Retirement Bill, Farm Bill, and Energy Bill, to name just three. In 2005, Congress set the stage for drilling by passing a budget bill, and in May 2006 the House voted yet again to open the Arctic Refuge to oil drilling, in spite of a major oil spill the previous March. And so it goes on and on in politics—against the wishes of the public, 70 percent of which disapproves of drilling in the refuge.

In the summer of 2006, fifty years after my initial visit, I returned to the Arctic National Wildlife Refuge on a trip initiated by the Murie Center in Jackson, Wyoming, and sponsored by the National Geographic Society, Wildlife Conservation Society, and Patagonia Company. Six of us, including writer Jon Waterman, University of Alaska professor Gary Kofinas, and three graduate students, rafted down the Canning River from the Brooks Range to the Arctic Ocean. We also visited Arctic Village to gain the insights of the Gwich'in people about climate change and their cultural dependence on caribou, and I talked to the children and grandchildren of Gwich'in I had met half a century before. Then we flew to the Sheenjek Valley, the site of the 1956 Murie expedition. We spent several days at our old camp by Last Lake, both a sentimental and a joyful return. In fifty years nothing had changed: even the golden eagle nest in a niche of a limestone cliff was still there. The Arctic Refuge retains its wildness, its "precious intangible values," as Olaus Murie phrased it.

Meanwhile the great caribou migration, currently about 120,000 animals strong, continues across the Arctic Refuge and into Canada's North Yukon National Park. The caribou are oblivious to their potential fate, but as the assault on the refuge goes on, so must our fight to save this national treasure.

On June 1, we established a tent camp at the base of a hillock. It commanded a view of a lake, still frozen except for a lead between ice and shore where muskrats splashed and old-squaw ducks paddled. Across the valley, beyond stands of stunted spruce, Table Mountain, in the Brooks Range, was capped with snow. On our hillock, however, the first purple saxifrages were in bloom, and beneath a rhododendron shrub a willow ptarmigan incubated her clutch of six eggs. White-rumped sandpipers, sanderlings, black-bellied plovers, and other shorebirds wheeled over the lake—migrants moving north through the heart of the Brooks Range to the coastal plain of the Arctic Ocean. Two grizzlies the color of winter grass traced the shoreline eating tender new sedges; round-shouldered and massive, they added a touch of tension to the scene.

A line of caribou crosses frozen Lobo Lake in front of our camp in the valley of the Sheenjek River. Photos in this chapter were taken during the summer of 1956.

Later that day a band of caribou crossed the lake in single file, their hooves clicking and whispering on the ice. Spring had returned to this Arctic valley and they with it, heading north and west to their summer grounds. In this season of twenty-four-hour daylight, even the night hours were filled with the songs of gray-cheeked thrushes, myrtle warblers, tree sparrows, and other species. And sometimes, far off, a Pacific loon gave its haunting call.

That was 1956. Our camp was situated north of the Yukon River flats, near where the Sheenjek River begins to penetrate the mountains. Years before, in 1938, Robert Marshall of the U.S. Forest Service had visited the Brooks Range—a limestone rampart across northern Alaska—and, enthralled by this wilderness, suggested: "It would seem desirable to establish a really sizable area free from roads and industries, where frontier conditions will be preserved." By the 1950s, northeastern Alaska was the last true wilderness in the United States, a vast ecosystem where caribou roamed unfettered and mountains rose in lonely grandeur. Indians—the Crow River Gwich'in—still inhabited the valleys south of the mountain crest, and Inuit tribes (the Nunamiut and the Tareumiut), the treeless expanses to the north. Today they are gone except for two small communities at the periphery of the area. Occasional hunters still penetrate the mountains in search of wolves, moose, and Dall sheep, but with time only the names of the rivers—the Kataturuk, Okpilak, Kongakut, Sheenjek, and others—will remain as memorials to these peoples.

Sponsored by the New York Zoological Society, we went to the Arctic in '56 to make the first biological survey of the region and to gather impressions of its "precious intangible values," as Olaus Murie, our expedition leader and president of the Wilderness Society, had phrased it. Also on the trip were Murie's wife, Margaret (Mardy), and biologists Brina Kessel and Robert Krear.

We traversed many mountains and nameless valleys to collect information. We pressed plants, made bird lists, examined places where grizzlies had turned sod in search of voles, and analyzed wolf and lynx droppings to determine what these predators had eaten. We learned

Olaus and Mardy Murie hike over the tundra near our camp at Last Lake in the Sheenjek Valley

much about the area. Each of us also received, in the words of Margaret Murie, "the gift of personal satisfaction, the personal well-being purchased by striving, by lifting and setting down legs over and over through muskeg, up the slopes, gaining the summit."

One day late in the summer, I set off on a lone weeklong walk to explore the headwaters of the Sheenjek. At 7,000 feet, I skirted a cirque glacier and then stood on a crest. Twelve Dall sheep rams were below, their coats bright against leaden scree, and beyond to the north the mountains sloped away toward the coastal plain. I descended to the headwaters of the East Fork of the Chandalar and there, very tired, unrolled my sleeping bag on a gravel bar.

A noise awakened me at 5:00 A.M.—a fused roar of rushing water and lowing cattle—and the ground vibrated as if in an earth tremor. Startled, I sat up.

Caribou! They filled the shadowed valley floor, flowing toward me like a wall of dark brown lava. I reclined again and waited. The animals continued onward and passed within sixty feet as if I were a mere log. Their pace was hectic, a mass of bulls, cows, and calves pushing down-valley, grunting, hooves churning gravel. A calf dropped behind its mother and bawled until she slowed her pace just a little. Bulls plodded with heads low beneath the weight of their antlers.

They had come from the coastal plain and across the divide. With ancient wisdom they now hurried eastward, moving, moving to the forested lowlands in Canada where they would winter. The clatter of hooves receded, and soon only a barnyard odor lingered in the calm air to attest to their passing. I dressed hurriedly.

Soon another wave washed toward me, and once more I transformed myself into a log. Another band of caribou came, and another—a total of about two thousand animals—all part of the Porcupine herd, as it is known, which numbers between 170,000 and 200,000. As the wildebeest define the Serengeti ecosystem, so do the caribou this region.

Our summer's work made it clear that northeastern Alaska deserved special protection. Olaus Murie took the lead in the long legislative battle to establish the Arctic National Wildlife Refuge. The bid to protect the wilderness made it through the House of Representatives, but, with Alaska's two senators opposed, it stalled in the Senate. Finally, by Executive Order on December 6, 1960, Secretary of the Interior Fred Seaton established the Arctic National Wildlife Range, an area of 8.9 million acres, slightly larger than the state of Vermont.

But within a few years—in 1968—oil companies announced a major oil strike at Prudhoe Bay, west of the reserve. The companies planned to drill for oil on the coastal plain and build a pipeline south across the mountains for eight hundred miles. Such development was bitterly fought by the conservation community, which argued that roads, pipelines, drilling pads, airstrips, garages, water treatment plants, and other development would destroy the wilderness character of the region. How could these things not damage an ecosystem so fragile that the track of even one cross-country vehicle remains visible for years? Despite protestations, President Richard Nixon authorized development of the Prudhoe oil field in 1973, and oil began to flow in 1977.

In 1980, President Jimmy Carter signed the Alaska National Interest Lands Conservation Act, which established 104 million acres of parks and reserves on federal lands. The Arctic National Wildlife *Refuge*, as it was renamed, was enlarged to 19 million acres.

Although the oil companies had already leased tens of millions of acres in northern Alaska, they coveted the coastal plain of the refuge as well, and in 1987 asked for drilling rights. They wanted only 1.5 million acres, they said, a mere 8 percent of the reserve's total area. The Department of Interior, under Secretary Donald Hodel, joined in promoting oil exploration in the refuge. The justification: U.S. dependence on foreign oil threatens national security. But the lack of a national energy strategy made conservationists skeptical of this appeal to "national security," especially because, in that same year, the Commerce Department issued a license to export Alaska crude oil produced at Cook Inlet. The arguments for and against drilling were clearly defined. The remote refuge, which few people have ever seen, became the

A curious lone caribou came to look at me as I crouched quietly to observe it.

country's conservation battleground for the 1980s . . . and perhaps for the '90s.

What are the facts? [Some minor details of the following may have changed since 1990.]

There is *at best* a 20 percent chance that oil would be found in economically recoverable amounts; a strike might produce from 0.6 to 9 billion barrels, with 3.2 billion barrels considered the most likely quantity. Even full-scale development might produce only enough oil to supply the country for a mere two hundred days.

While raising the specter of national security, the government simultaneously lowered auto gas mileage standards, raised rural high-way speed limits, and slashed funds for research into alternative energy sources. A modest increase in auto fuel efficiency alone would save more oil than the supposed total output of the Arctic National Wildlife Refuge.

The coastal plain of the refuge is the age-old calving ground of the Porcupine herd. Female caribou accompanied by young are known to avoid roads and pipelines, and calf mortality might increase if they were forced to bear their young in less favorable areas. A decline in the caribou population would diminish one of the Earth's great wildlife spectacles. Canada has a 2.5-million-acre national park on its side of the border, and by international agreement, the two nations have pledged to conserve the caribou.

Oil companies claim that drilling would result in only modest ecological damage. Yet Prudhoe Bay has an average of five hundred oil spills a year. In 1986, 64 million gallons of wastewater containing toxic metals and chemicals were discharged directly onto the tundra. Emissions of nitrogen oxide and sulfur dioxide, components of acid rain, rival in amount those of Chicago. Wolves and grizzlies have disappeared with hunting. Oil companies are supposed to restore damaged environment but so far have not.

Wilderness reserves are created not for their economic value but as statements of a nation's vision and identity. Sadly, no place in the United States appears to be safe from the demands of exploiters, not even reserves. As a result of the *Exxon Valdez* disaster, both the government and the oil companies lightened the pressure to drill for oil in the Arctic National Wildlife Refuge. But the Persian Gulf crisis has served as an excuse to make that pressure stronger than ever. This case may yet verify the desolate axiom that conservation yields no victories, only postponement of defeat, no matter how loud the cries of protest by those who care.

One oil company executive called the refuge "a flat, crummy place. Only for oil would anybody want to go up there." He exemplifies a U.S. addiction to exploiting, squandering, destroying. Fortunately there are people of vision, too. Author Wallace Stegner wrote: "Something will have gone out of us as a people if we ever let the remaining wilderness be destroyed... if we pollute the last clean air and dirty the last clean streams and push our paved roads through the last of the silence."

Should the Arctic National Wildlife Refuge be permanently scarred for a few days of oil? Should the Serengeti become a cattle ranch? Should the Grand Canyon be dammed?

[1990]

Raising Siegfried

Great Blue Heron

While at the University of Alaska from 1951 to 1955, I spent long summers in the field learning to be a naturalist. I followed caribou on migration in central Alaska, studied birds on the tundra of the Arctic slope, and took part in a biological survey of Katmai National Monument. In my coursework, I was exposed to the study of animal behavior, or ethology, which involves making detailed descriptions of what animals do and interpreting the meaning of such behavior in their society and in evolution.

Later, John Emlen, a well-known ornithologist at the University of Wisconsin, accepted me as one of his graduate students. The first task he gave me was to study the development of fear in young birds. At what age does a bird begin to avoid strange stimuli? I hatched chickens, pheasants, ducklings, and other species from eggs, and I visited the nests of robins, grackles, and bluebirds around the campus to monitor the development of nestlings. I presented them all with various objects, from colored pieces of cardboard to a rubber owl, to note their responses at various ages. I had a room that was in effect my private aviary, where ducklings followed me like a mother, as so delightfully described first by Konrad Lorenz—and I also had two herons.

Students of animal behavior have in recent years become greatly interested in tracing the development of behavior patterns in young animals,

37

especially birds. Scientists try to determine, among other things, to what extent various actions are inborn, and how learning affects them in the course of the animal's growth.

When on May 10, at 4:20 P.M., a great blue heron wriggled from his egg onto the wire tray of my incubator at the University of Wisconsin, he was far removed from the influences that would have shaped his behavior in the wild. As Siegfried, which I later called him although I never knew his sex, struggled and kicked in an attempt to raise his rubbery neck, he saw not a nest of sticks high in the crown of an elm—which was his natural home in a rookery in southeastern Wisconsin—but only the confining walls of a room; he saw no adult herons landing with rushing wings at the edge of the swaying nest, but only a man standing by his nest box.

However, Siegfried had no vision of the proper state of affairs. His only concern was for food—a voracious concern that changed him from a two-ounce weakling at birth to a two-pound fighter at three weeks.

Immediately after emerging from the egg, his gray down plastered wetly to his plump body and his scrawny neck lacking the strength to hold up his head, Siegfried emitted his food call, a rasping *kek-kek*. By the following morning he could raise his head and feebly lunge with open beak at pieces of liver I dangled in front of him. After grasping a piece between the mandibles, he threw back his head as would an adult heron and swallowed.

His grabbing for food was inaccurate, and he missed as often as not. But when something stimulated the lining of his bill, he showed a curious behavior. As if someone had flipped the switch of his internal motor, he lunged and lunged, five to ten times, at nothing in particular. If a leaf or branch inadvertently landed in his bill, he tried to swallow that too, and I had to be careful to eliminate all small objects from the nest. This chain reaction of swallowing is undoubtedly useful when the helpless youngster is fed a mass of regurgitated food by his parent in the wild.

After a meal Siegfried rested, stretched out, looking like a fuzzy, long-necked gourd.

When Siegfried and his
nest mate met at nine days
of age, he immediately
asserted his dominance,
grabbing his sister's bill
and twisting it until she
fell on her side.

Siegfried sees his reflection in a mirror held by Kay, and his ire is evident from his raised crest.

By the age of five days he had changed to an alert youngster. He sat on his haunches for the first time, though he was somewhat wobbly and barely balanced on his rounded belly. He watched avidly as I prepared his food, and he pecked at spots and shiny objects within reach. Interestingly, now that he could peck with precision, his automatic lunging for food had all but disappeared.

I had also been raising one of Siegfried's nest mates, a female as it later turned out, in the same room but out of his sight. I put the two herons together for the first time on May 18, anticipating an amicable meeting. But both sat rigidly upright, facing one another with wings spread and with neck and bill stretched skyward. The pinfeathers on their necks stood erect like quills, and the long tufts of down on cheeks and crown flared outward, giving the young herons the appearance of angry old men with side-whiskers.

After briefly holding this adultlike threat posture, they emitted some loud, sharp *cau-cau* calls, indicating annoyance; then they jabbed at each other's head with rapierlike thrusts of their bills. Siegfried grabbed the bill of his sister and twisted it sideways until she fell on her side. He then aimed a few more jabs at his downed victim, handling his bill like a sword. It was for this flashing bill that I named him Siegfried, after a hero of German legend who had a magic sword.

Like many other birds, herons apparently have no inherited means by which they can recognize others of their own species. By the age of eight days Siegfried had learned that I was his parent. Once recognition was established, he accepted no other animals, whether dogs, chickens, or other members of his species.

On May 24, I again attempted to put the two herons together. They immediately assumed their threatening posture, and Siegfried started to jab at his sister. But he only clapped his bill, and when his sister responded in similar fashion, he bowed down, touching the ground with the tip of his bill as if in submissiveness. However, as before, the meeting ended with the herons hammering away at each other.

One project occupied Siegfried for the next few weeks: learning to stand up. At the age of two weeks he rose from his haunches for the first time, but his bottom was so heavy that it pulled him back down. Thereafter, until he could stand like an adult, he maintained his upright position in two ways: he either leaned far forward and, like a tripod, balanced himself by touching the tip of his bill to the ground, or he stood bolt upright, resembling an animated wine bottle.

Siegfried's voracious hunger never abated. When I came into the room he danced up and down, beat his wings while throwing his snake-like neck back and forth, and roared in a most ferocious manner. Feeding was now an easy matter: I simply dropped a whole perch or rat down his gullet and watched it slowly slide down the distended neck. Bones and skin were later regurgitated in a pellet.

Satiated, Siegfried huddled close to me, emitting soft, musical *ka-kas*. He sometimes preened my bare arms with a rapid sideways movement of the head, and when I picked him up, he rested his neck over my shoulder. Yet, unlike a duckling, he never followed when I moved away from him. The tendency to follow would be fatal to a flightless heron in a treetop. Not until June 17, when he was well feathered out, did Siegfried step from his nest box onto the table on which it sat.

Although he usually tolerated other persons, Siegfried seemed ill at ease with them—and they with him—for he lashed out at their faces on occasion. When I took him out-of-doors, he stood motionless, like a post, his gray-blue plumage blending into the surroundings. If a stranger inadvertently wandered close to him, he suddenly turned into a feathered fury, roaring and running at the intruder with clapping bill, spread wings, and ruffled feathers. It was a stout soul who stood his ground.

On July 28, after a heavy rainstorm, I carried him to a large puddle, the first he had seen. He stared into the water as if remembering his

Siegfried took to the water readily when he was released at a nearby lake.

heritage. In a flash he jabbed at a pebble below the surface of the water, held it to the ground, and "killed" it by shaking his head rapidly. The heron's method of obtaining prey had appeared in its full form without previous experience.

In mid-July, Siegfried felt independence coming upon him and began to break the social bonds that linked him to me. Previously, he had enjoyed being scratched, but now he drew away from me; instead of permitting me to feed him by hand, he preferred to pick up his own food; rather than welcoming the chance to be carried, he scolded me. Perched at the edge of his nest, he beat his powerful wings in practice and occasionally leaped five feet to another part of the room. On July 28, he flew for the first time, low over the ground but in typical adult fashion, with stately wingbeats and folded neck.

The time had come for Siegfried to gain his freedom. I had learned much from him. He had shown me that many of his actions, even complex ones like threat displays and prey-killing movements, were largely inherited, but that learning may play an important role, as in species recognition.

On August 11, when he was three months old, I took him to a marsh where reeds grew densely and open leads of water would provide good fishing for a heron. He stood in the shallows, neck poised for a strike, watching minnows scurry away, as if he had done this all his life. His inscrutable face betrayed in no way that he was in a strange place. As always, his mind was on food. I felt that he could survive on his own. When I walked away, he flew up and circled above me before landing at my feet. Again I carried him into the marsh, then hurried away.

Little did I know Siegfried's restless soul. The following day he landed on a house about twenty miles to the northwest of the marsh and was identified by the number of the band on his leg. And on the same day he was reported forty miles to the west—a fine flight for a bird that had never before flown farther than a few hundred feet. I never heard of him again.

[1967]

Author's note: *Birds may have little trouble adapting to the wild after being in captivity. After all, starlings, house sparrows, and ring-necked pheasants, to name just three, were introduced into the United States, and rehabilitation programs for various species from Bali mynahs to peregrine falcons have been successful. I wished Siegfried good fishing and a long, congenial life.*

Glories of Another World

Rainforest

Once I accompanied several Yanomamo Indians through the Amazon rainforest toward the Neblina highlands, on the border between Brazil and Venezuela. For days we had hiked and then climbed, until the ancient trees gave way to shrub and meadow, and below us the forest canopy billowed far to the horizon. These Indians had spent their lives in forest gloom and now, for the first time, they took in an immense view. They leaped and waved their arms and whooped with joy. I could understand their elation: landscapes of light and space affect me similarly.

That Amazon journey was in 1977. I wonder how long the forest world of these Indians will survive, even though part of it has been reserved for them by the Brazilian government. In 2004 alone Brazil felled ten thousand square miles of rainforest for timber, cattle ranches, and agriculture. Appeals to save the glorious biodiversity there and elsewhere are failing largely because landowners and businesses have little incentive to care for natural assets such as forests, water, and arable land.

We must strive for coexistence with nature, to balance development with the long-term good of the land and its people. What will motivate us to conserve something for tomorrow? One approach is economic. The Forest Stewardship Council gives a seal of approval to timber that is logged selectively, thereby encouraging eco-minded consumers to buy it at a premium. Certified shade-grown, bird-friendly coffee, raised beneath the forest canopy, is already available at a higher price. In this age of global markets, something similar ought to be *done with cattle, soybeans, wheat, palm oil, and other products that stimulate ever more forest destruction. Environmental tax and other credits can be given to landowners who save critical habitat, manage water and wetlands, and conserve other resources. Such innovative economic approaches offer just one remedy to the careless squandering of valuable resources.*

Tomorrow is almost here for the Yanomamo Indians—and for all of us.

A rainforest can change one's perception of life. Its massive trees, crowded with epiphytes and swerving lianas, and its humid warmth engulf an intruder. Everything is lush, serene, brooding; there is no horizon, no sky. Here is the greatest celebration of life our planet has ever seen. To be surrounded by a million species is exhilarating, yet even to a naturalist like myself, such luxuriance is difficult to comprehend, almost intimidating. I come from a temperate climate, from the fringe of biological diversity, where life seems spacious and exposed.

Rainforest animals are furtive, filled with secrets and solitudes. In the Amazon, a group of howler monkeys may proclaim the dawn with voices that, like the approach of a storm, fuse into a loud roar. Then, silence. Or a line of three-toed tracks may trace the edge of a slough— the tracks of a capybara, the world's largest rodent, but the imagination conjures a small dinosaur to fit the primal scene. Such contacts add to a feeling of isolation. A cluster of orange-colored *Dryas* butterflies on an ocelot dropping provides a rare flash of visual delight, as well as an appreciation of nature's complexity: they are all males in search of salts in the dropping, which they will later transfer with their sperm to females. The forest itself provides no sense of recognition. A hundred tree species may crowd on an acre.

Because of its overpowering size, a rainforest requires close examination; its beauty lies in the detail. Seen from the ground, most birds are fleeting silhouettes in the canopy, difficult to identify and a strain on the neck. To be near such birds, I climbed a giant *Anisoptera* tree near Kuala

The Amazon rainforest rises into the Neblina highlands, on the border between northern Brazil and Venezuela.

Lumpur in Malaysia. As I ascended to a precarious platform, the air became brighter, warmer, and drier, an environment different from that in the shadows below. Here, 140 feet above the forest floor, *Draco* lizards glided among the branches, and mixed flocks of scarlet minivets, fairy bluebirds, green iornis, and others searched the foliage around me for insects. The rainforest is a three-dimensional world unlike any other, its layered canopy and many tree species offering orchids, ferns, and bromeliads a roof garden, and animals innumerable niches in which to feed and hide.

An intriguing aspect of rainforest life is its extraordinary mutualism, a dependence of organisms upon each other. For instance, each of the many fig species has its own wasp pollinators. Fruit-eating birds, fish, and especially bats disperse the seeds. How wonderful to visualize bats on velvet wings swooping over forest clearings softly sowing seeds in the darkness. A rainforest is remarkably complex, yet its stability is tenuous. The extinction of a pollinator or seed disperser may cause the death of a plant species and with it many other species, especially invertebrates,

The black curassow is a familiar species in the Amazon forests, much favored by indigenous people for food.

which depend on it. Such responses are subtle and perhaps long delayed. How many key species can a rainforest lose before order becomes chaos, before the community collapses in an avalanche of extinctions?

Although biology is at the forefront of science today, tropical ecology is in its infancy. We are still ignorant of most biological processes. We know little about where most biodiversity is and lack adequate techniques to inventory it. Indeed most species of invertebrates remain unknown, anonymous. What determines species abundance? Various theories have been proposed, including levels of soil fertility and speciation in refugia during the Pleistocene, when temperatures were lower and the forests fragmented. The laws of biological evolution—genetic variation and natural selection—are probably incomplete without adding the physical and chemical systems of air and soil. The rainforest, which Charles Darwin called the "glories of another world," can provide basic new insights.

Species diversity in the rainforest became reality for me one November night by the Madeirinha River in the Amazon. Day and night, a huge floating dredge sifted the sand and silt for diamonds. Bright lights illuminated the night work, and these were almost obscured by swarms of moths so varied in size, color, and structure that even a casual count revealed more than fifty species.

The dredge was also a reminder that just as we become aware of the splendor of the rainforest, we are in danger of losing it. More than half of our rainforests have been cut during this century, and such destruction is accelerating. An estimated nineteen million trees are felled *daily*. How many species have already been lost? The rainforests have become a battleground between those who want short-term gain and those who decry the ethos of greed and indifference with which our biodiversity is casually squandered. Ranchers cut century-old trees to make short-lived cattle pastures; developers, often with international cooperation, destroy forests by building roads, hydroelectric dams, and mines; and loggers denude the landscape with cut-and-run practices. Pillaging pays. The cost is borne by society, nature, and the future. Much old-growth forest is also being destroyed by slash-and-burn cultivators, some who have occupied a region for centuries and others who are poor immigrants in search of a plot of land.

Politicians and policy makers like to give benefits, not impose restraints; they are concerned with immediate gain, not long-term issues. Arguments on behalf of rainforest conservation, whether climatic stability, watershed protection, or the potential economic value of species, tend to be ignored in favor of development. It seems to me that human survival, even if promoted by self-interest, is a good argument for saving rainforests. These forests are nature's greatest pharmacy and supermarket, the genes of which will provide us with new foods and drugs. We cannot predict which species, perhaps insignificant, will ultimately be essential to us. It is a sad reflection on current attitudes that conservationists must argue why something should be saved instead of exploiters explaining why it should be destroyed.

We desperately need plans for the environment, not just development to supply us with resources. It has even been suggested that all wilderness areas, including reserves, be simply turned over to local peoples on the mistaken and romantic notion that they live in harmony with nature. As the archaeological record shows, native peoples have often abused their own environment. Today half of all forest destruction is caused by shifting cultivators. True, if people are few, there is no commercial incentive, technology is simple, and social restraints exist; then, indeed, the environmental impact can be modest. However, such peoples have almost vanished; isolation is not possible in the modern world. Traditional lives have usually unraveled under the stress of market forces, a desire for consumer products, and rising expectations.

Can a rainforest be harvested sustainably? So far no commercial logging has been sustainable. And reforestation is not an easy solution; we can plant trees but cannot re-create the original forest. Ecological processes are so complicated that planted forests are only superficial replicas. Community-based conservation efforts have emphasized agroforestry, in which people raise a variety of crops—from bananas to cashews—on small plots, gather such forest produce as rubber and Brazil nuts, and practice aquaculture in the rivers, all while preserving much of the forest canopy. Over time, an economy based on gathering forest products can yield more than twice the income of logging or cattle ranching. However, proponents of sustainable development seldom mention limits—limits on the number of persons in an area, on the number of monkeys killed for food, on the amount of forest degraded. Without enforced limits, there can be no sustainability. Who makes the decisions about access to resources and amounts that may be extracted so that harvest rates do not exceed production? Who can make such complicated decisions? We still know too little to manipulate forests and predict the consequences.

Often a forest still looks pristine but certain species have been harvested so intensively that they are locally extinct or rare. In Myanmar, I met rattan collectors working deep in the forest because all easily

A Tamandua *anteater peers at me from the safety of a tree in Brazil.*

accessible stems of this climbing palm had long been depleted for the global market. In northern Brazil, I walked for several days through the forest with Yanomamo Indians. Instead of carrying traditional bows and arrows, they brought shotguns—with shells sold by a local mission. We did not see or hear any large monkeys, and I was told that most had been shot within a radius of more than a day's walk from the Yanomamo village. But a community such as this, with its culture relatively intact, could with some help design a management plan that would enable it to harvest wildlife sustainably. A Machiguenga Indian community in Peru's Manu National Park has already accomplished this. However, if a local population hunts for the market without restraint, certain species will be rapidly depleted, as studies have shown from Sarawak and Gabon to Venezuela. Yet even commercial use can be sustained if the local community is involved in the conservation process and limits are accepted. In Brazil's Mamirauá Reserve on the Amazon, fishermen have done just that.

From a conservation perspective, only one measure is valid: is biodiversity being preserved? It is unfashionable these days to talk of protecting areas, of limiting access and use. If logging and agricultural practices were less primitive and wasteful, and if degraded lands were used more efficiently for crops, livestock, fuelwood, and tree plantations, no more old-growth forests would have to be cleared. Perhaps this will be accomplished in the future, but action is imperative now. Every nation must protect as much of its biodiversity as possible in a network of large reserves, in cooperation with the local population. Decisions about saving biodiversity are made far from forests by governments. Therefore, protection has to be based on laws and sanctified by society.

No comprehensive solution to rainforest destruction is possible until we treat the root causes. One cause is population growth; another is international debt. Poor countries try to repay loans to overdeveloped countries like Japan and the United States by logging their forests and growing export crops. And the consumer nations buy these resources at unfairly low prices without concern for the social consequences and environmental degradation to much of the world.

Any naturalist is all too aware of nature's wounds. My reflections on rainforest conservation are of the kind that constantly invade my mind when I am afield. During a recent visit to Laos, I marveled at some of the fine forest tracts. But vast areas have also been denuded by slash-and-burn cultivators. Proposed dams would inundate some of the remaining forests. Convoys of trucks carrying logs destined for Japan head east toward the South China Sea. Poachers are eliminating the last tigers and elephants, species often considered natural icons. Bushmeat fills the local markets with everything from squirrel to sambar, as well as brilliant bouquets of dead forest birds.

We all have a huge stake in the survival of rainforests such as those in Laos. Humankind is losing its options for the future, but it is not yet ready to make painful choices; it does not yet feel threatened by the loss of species. Denial is much easier. Perhaps during the coming century we will, with an outburst of common sense, become enlightened and protect the remnants of our natural treasures. We will, I hope, recognize that mutualism, so basic to rainforest plants and animals, extends to humans as well, that we remain a part of and not separate from the natural world. The environmental crisis cannot be resolved by science and politics alone. It is a moral issue, determined by culture and character. We need a change in attitude, consciousness, priorities, and expectations, a new strategy for human survival that decries waste and destruction and places a spiritual value on caring for the natural world.

[1998]

The Mouse That Barks

Capybara

I was intrigued and enchanted by my first brief meetings with capybaras in *Argentina, but learned little about them then. Later, in 1978 and 1979, when I studied jaguars in the great swamps of the Mato Grosso in Brazil, I often observed capybaras during the dry season, when they would concentrate by the few remaining pools along the Trans-Pantanal Highway. I tarried to watch them day after day and soon recognized several distinct groups, most with five to twenty members. Each had settled in a certain area of about thirty to a hundred acres in size, where the animals grazed, bathed, and loafed the hot noon hours away in the shade of a bush. The groups were stable, some with just one adult male and one female and others with an adult male and a harem of females. The adult male defended a territory against intruding males by chasing them and trying to lacerate them with his large, curved incisors. A few groups contained several adults of both sexes, and in addition, there were roaming groups of males only. The species has a flexible social system, useful in a habitat with drastic seasonal changes, when pastures are either flooded or baked dry, to which the animals have to adapt.*

To sit and observe these giant rodents was the kind of peaceful indulgence of a private passion that had attracted me to the life of a naturalist.

We humans like our environment predictable, with everything fitting into the established order of things: science fiction is expected to remain a fantasy. It is disconcerting, therefore, to meet a 150-pound mouse, especially one that barks like a dog and wallows like a pig.

I met my first capybara in Argentina while visiting a ranch. The owner was partial to these huge rodents, and about three hundred of them thrived there around a series of ponds. In the morning, while walking along the shores, I encountered capybaras by the dozens, sitting or foraging, their rotund bodies supported on spindly legs. With only a rudimentary tail, an outsized broad head, and a blunt nose that looks like it was shaped by running full tilt into a brick wall, the capybara has an unfinished look, as if its creator failed to add some final touches. Its sparse and scraggly coat, reddish brown in color, has a bargain-basement quality.

The capybara most closely resembles a guinea pig—but a guinea pig forty inches long and twenty inches high at the shoulder. Both rodents belong to the suborder *Hystricomorpha,* as do porcupines and chinchillas. This suborder of rodents differs from the squirrels and ratlike animals in the shape of the mandible and other minor anatomical characteristics. Hystricomorphs are an old group, present at least since the Oligocene Epoch. They had their most marked evolutionary radiation in South America, where they appropriated ecological niches often used by hoofed animals on other continents.

Although widely distributed throughout their range in the lowlands from Panama to Argentina, capybaras are infrequently seen in the wild. Searching for them along forest-fringed rivers and in marshes, I found their three-toed tracks, like those of a big bird, and saw their droppings, as large as those of a moose. But the animals themselves remained elusive, skulking in thickets. Having no den, they seek refuge in water when disturbed, and there hide themselves by silently submerging, leaving only their nostrils and eyes above the surface. One could conclude that the species is by nature nocturnal, but it is not.

Capybaras have good reasons for being cryptic. In Argentina, they say, "Anything that walks ends up on a skewer." Everywhere, capybaras are hunted for their meat and hides. Several ranches in Venezuela even

Various birds, including the cattle tyrant, like to perch on capybara and search their hides, presumably for insects.

raise them commercially, the first sustained effort at game ranching for meat in South America. However, *capybara en brochette* has so far not become a conspicuous item on menus. Some ranchers are loath to harbor capybaras because the species is a wild reservoir for equine trypanosomiasis, a deadly disease of horses. Yet in spite of almost continuous harassment, the animals have endured and, in fact, have done so well that they are one of the few large mammals in South America that is not endangered. But to succeed they had to change their habits in the wild; thus, in the face of human pressure, they became nocturnal and shy.

On the ranch I visited, the capybaras were safe from hunting, and consequently they behaved in a normal manner, being active and conspicuous for much of the day. I took advantage of this opportunity to make some preliminary observations of their behavior. Except for a fine ecological study by Juhani Ojasti in Venezuela, little work has been done on capybaras in the wild.

A capybara rests in reeds, its long incisors clearly visible.

Capybaras are often thought to be aquatic, and indeed their existence revolves around water, even their toes being partially webbed. However, water mainly represents safety, a place into which they retreat in times of danger. For much of the day the animals are on land, feeding and resting. They forage in the mornings until after 8:30 or so, when more and more animals settle down to rest. Although they occasionally eat aquatic plants, their main diet consists of grass. Leisurely waddling along, they nip the tender shoots with their long white incisors. Their molars are rootless and ever-growing, a useful adaptation for an animal that seasonally may have to live on coarse forage.

As I walked along the well-beaten capybara trails, the animals usually spotted me and sat erect, their lower lips in a petulant droop. Suddenly, one or more barked, a yippy sound like that of a small dog, and all bounded toward one of the ponds. Giving a leap, they dove head-first, hitting the water with an explosive splash. I suspect that this splash functions as a danger signal similar to the slap of a beaver's tail hitting the water before a dive. After swimming some 50 to 150 feet beneath the surface, they popped up to survey the situation. Everything being safe, they smoothly and gracefully swam back to shore, only the tops of their heads above the surface. Such a watery retreat is useful when eluding predators like humans, jaguars, and pumas—but not caimans and anacondas. The selective forces that shape behavior generally present an animal with a compromise to a problem, rather than a solution.

Midday is siesta time. Like bundles of unkempt fur, the capybaras loll around, some on the grass, others in the shade of trees. Some wallow in mud, alone or communally, with as many as twenty squeezed together like some bemuddled encounter group. In 1776, Linnaeus gave capybaras the scientific name *Sus hydrochaeris*, pig of the water. Although the capybara is no relative of the pig and its name is now *Hydrochaerus hydrochaeris*, the old designation suited the animal because of its swinelike passion for lounging in mud. These wallows no doubt assist in keeping the capybara cool and also prevent the skin, with its scanty hair cover, from burning in the sun. The animals rest until about 3:30 to 4:00 P.M. and then resume their foraging.

Sometimes I reclined on the grass while the capybaras pottered nearby. When at ease, they emit a soft clicking sound, perhaps indicating to others that all is well. As I lay looking up at the rodents, I felt like a strayed Lilliputian among a colony of field mice. While so close to them, I tried to discover something about their social life. One problem in studying capybaras is that the sexes look so much alike. Males and females are about equal in size, weighing an average of 110 pounds as adults, with some as much as 150 pounds. However, at the age of about one year, males develop a shiny black growth, a fatty gland, on top of their muzzle. The males rub this gland on vegetation, depositing a musky odor that may stimulate other animals to mark the same place. They also use another marking technique: walking along, a male or female will purposely step over a tuft of grass or leafy branch, letting the vegetation slide between its hind legs, thereby depositing secretions from the paired anal glands.

Capybara are social, living in both small and large herds.

Do all members of a population recognize each other by scent, evicting strangers from the home ground? I don't know. I saw groups of various sizes, some small, only a female or two with their young, others with twenty, thirty, or, in one instance, sixty-four individuals together. In 1802, the explorer Alexander von Humboldt met a group of about one hundred. But such groups are not stable in composition, the animals joining and parting at intervals. Males are often solitary. At the Evansville Zoo in Indiana, it was found that two males could not be kept together, for they slashed at each other with chattering teeth. Females there occasionally killed each other's young. But this may have been due to confinement. In the wild, up to a dozen young—the progeny of several females—may huddle together in a nursery. As we have a pod of pelicans, do we now have a cuddle of capybaras?

Capybaras breed throughout the year in Venezuela, with a peak of mating shortly before the onset of the main rainy season in April and May. I saw courtship in October in Argentina, also just prior to the rains. A courting male follows the female closely, his nose almost touching her rump. Entering water, she may dive, he still following behind, then plod into the shallows, where she slows down or halts, permitting him to mount. Several males may mate with a female in succession, according to Ojasti. The gestation period is not accurately known: some say 104 to 111 days, some 119 to 126 days, and still others 149 to 156 days. In any event, from two to eight young—usually two to five—are born, each weighing three or four pounds. The young are precocial, able to follow their mother and eat grass soon after birth.

As a zoologist, I viewed the capybaras on the Argentina ranch with special interest. Here is a rodent that, unlike other rodents, normally leads a conspicuous life in the open, a life resembling that of many hoofed animals, such as deer and antelope. I wondered how the capybara had adapted to this change. Did it take up the lifestyle of a hoofed animal? In some of its behavior, such as its method of anal marking, the capybara remains a typical Hystricomorph. But unlike rodents, it forms herds, which forage, rest, and flee together; it keeps in contact by vocalizing softly like a sounder of pigs; the young are sometimes in nurseries, as is the case among elk; and it gives loud alarm barks. This huge rodent may help us gain fascinating insights into the ecological pressures that help shape societies. But above all, it is an appealing creature whose presence adds a unique distinction to South America's vanishing wilderness.

[1976]

Stalking the Pantanal

Jaguar

My studies of various animals were first attempts to enter their lives. Any biography begins with a gathering of small facts, each of which contributes a new insight, whether the contents of a scat or a brief social interaction. After I moved on to other lands and other species, many biologists enlarged upon my initial efforts, resulting in a much greater depth of knowledge. Although my understanding of animals always remained incomplete, I treasured my time with them, and so it was with the jaguar.

After most of our study animals were killed by ranch hands in 1978, as described in this article, we established a new base farther south in the Pantanal on the Miranda ranch, where the Klabin family welcomed us. Peter Crawshaw and Howard Quigley continued the jaguar study between 1980 and 1984, radio-tracking six jaguars whose ranges were large—each about sixty square miles—and overlapping. Work still continues in the Pantanal, especially on the conflict between jaguars and ranchers, who dislike the cats because they occasionally kill cattle. In 1983, Alan Rabinowitz of the Wildlife Conservation Society initiated a project in the rainforest of Belize, where jaguars have small ranges of only about fifteen square miles and subsist mostly on small prey, such as armadillos. Alan's efforts resulted in the establishment of Latin America's first jaguar reserve, the Cockscomb Wildlife Sanctuary. Soon jaguar studies in Paraguay, Bolivia, Peru, Mexico, Venezuela, and Costa Rica contributed greatly to information about the cat's natural history. The Wildlife Conservation Society has now developed an action plan to protect and monitor the species *throughout its range from Argentina to the southern border of the United States.*

Large carnivores, such as the jaguars, tend to exist at low densities and in small populations, making them blueprints for local extinction. However, they have important ecological functions, helping to structure the ecosystem through their impact on prey, on other carnivore species, and ultimately on the vegetation. The removal of jaguars may have a far-reaching and unanticipated impact on the whole habitat. To help a species endure, we need good science, sound policy, and public support, all of which large carnivores tend to lack.

Footprints in the mud told the story. During the night a female jaguar, screened by a bush at the edge of the bay, had stalked a capybara, pounced on it, and killed it in a flurry of violence before it could escape to the safety of deep water. Then, straddling the seventy-five-pound rodent with her forelegs, she had picked it up in her jaws and hauled it across the beach into the forest.

I followed the drag mark into a wilderness of thorns, wending my way through stiletto-like bromeliads and past spiny lianas. One step at a time I advanced, listening intently. My eyes tried to penetrate the black hollows between the bushes ahead, and I willed the hidden jaguar to reveal itself. Surely she knew of my presence, for the fallen leaves of the August dry season crackled underfoot. Perhaps she had abandoned the prey after a hasty meal, something jaguars often do.

Then, just ahead, a low, continuous growl warned me to stop. Slowly I knelt, hoping for a glint of the luminous black-speckled hide beneath the shadowy bushes where she crouched by her kill. But she remained invisible. Not wanting to disturb her further, I retraced my steps, foiled once again in my efforts to see her. For several months I had been studying jaguars in Brazil, mostly on the Acurizal ranch, which covers fifty-five square miles from the floodplains of the Paraguay River westward to the Serra de Amolar, a high ridge along the Bolivian border.

A jaguar, with its radio-collar just visible, hides in dense vegetation.

During this time I became distantly familiar with the jaguars there by following their round pugmarks along cattle trails and beaches, and by examining their kills. To identify individuals by their paw prints is not difficult when only a few inhabit an area. The pugmarks of an adult male can be distinguished from those of a female by their larger size, rounder shape, and greater spread of the toes; the prints of a young animal are smaller than those of an adult, and they may be with or near those of a female. When two females occupy the same range it can be difficult to identify their tracks, but they usually have some distinguishing characteristic, such as a slight peculiarity in the shape of the heel pad.

At Acurizal I found that two jaguars, a female and her presumed fifteen- to eighteen-month-old daughter, hunted through a fifteen-square-mile area of forest. The open woodlands provided them with cattle—their principal prey—and patches of dense secondary growth were favored retreats of the white-lipped peccary, another important

To reach isolated forest islands in the swamps in search of jaguar, we poled a boat through the floating vegetation of water hyacinths. The Pantanal, one of the world's largest freshwater wetland systems, is now partly protected by a national park.

food species. Strips of gallery forest bordered two streams draining the Serra, and these sheltered other prey, such as brocket deer and tapirs. It was cellar-cool under the trees, and jaguars often rested there during the heat of the day. A third female visited Acurizal intermittently, her range partly overlapping that of the other two. And, finally, a medium-sized male not only claimed the ranch as his own, but also extended his travels into forests to the west.

This land-tenure system—with territories of neighboring females overlapping and the range of a resident male including several females—is similar to that of other large solitary cats. Although part of a community in which members monitor each other's doings, jaguars, like tigers and pumas, essentially live alone. Judging by their tracks, even the female and grown daughter seldom associated. On one occasion, the male and the mother traveled together, perhaps because she was in heat. Peter Crawshaw, my Brazilian coworker, tracked the two of them to where they had killed a collared anteater—playfully, it seemed, for they merely bit the animal through the back before abandoning it.

The morning after the female growled at me, I left camp to walk a grassy beach between waterline and forest, once more seeking to meet her. To my right stretched the Pantanal, a 40,000-square-mile swampy plain that is partly flooded each year by the Paraguay River and its tributaries. This mosaic of forests, marshes, lakes, and sloughs harbors one of the great wildlife concentrations in South America. After a visit to the area in 1912, Theodore Roosevelt wrote, "It is literally an ideal place in which a field naturalist could spend six months or a year." Now, sixty-four years later, I was in the Pantanal hoping not only to study its wildlife but also to encourage the Brazilian government to establish a national park there.

Several black vultures rose from the thicket where the female had dragged her capybara kill. After eating only parts of the forequarters— the brisket, heart, liver, and one shoulder—she had abandoned the remains. In this climate a capybara is edible for no more than two or three days, after which the meat becomes rotten and maggoty. Yet jaguars, even when undisturbed, often spend only one night with a carcass. Perhaps food is so plentiful that the cats do not worry about their next meal, especially since their menu includes not just capybaras and hoofed stock but a wide variety of other creatures: fish, tortoises, anacondas, caimans, coatis, otters, and howler monkeys.

A swarm of flies followed as I dragged the carcass from the thicket. As usual, the cat had killed the capybara with a neat bite into the skull. The jaguar takes the head into its mouth and, with its opposing canines, punctures the bone to the brain. This technique is noteworthy not only for the precision with which the canines pierce the skull on or near the ears but also for the strength needed to penetrate half an inch of bone.

Jaguars may even kill cows by crunching open their skulls, using a primitive force alien to lions and tigers, which usually dispatch large prey more fastidiously by strangulation.

Each day some thirty to thirty-five capybaras grazed along a five-mile stretch of beach where the jaguars often hunted. What effect did predation have on these giant rodents?

To find out we walked the beach almost daily for two months searching for fresh kills. The cats killed seven capybaras in that time, a fifth of this small population. The impact of such predation was obviously so great that these rodents could not long survive the pressure. However, this finding must be viewed in historical perspective. Many hundreds of capybaras existed in the area until 1974, when a severe flood submerged much of their habitat near the Paraguay River. The animals crowded along the water's edge, where they soon began to die of disease—most likely horse sickness, a form of trypanosomiasis. The parasite, for which these rodents are natural hosts, probably was quiescent in the animals until the stress of crowding and lack of food caused it to become virulent.

The area was still flooded at the time of our study in 1977, and disease still affected the capybaras. Four animals in our sample were near death, emaciated and covered with sores, and several others were ill.

Normally, capybaras can tolerate disease and predation, for they are prolific breeders. Each female produces a litter of up to eight at least once a year, but for unknown reasons few young were born or survived at Acurizal. Thus, decimated by illness and hampered by a low rate of reproduction, the population could not absorb the additional stress of predation. Fortunately for the capybaras, the jaguars soon switched their hunting to another part of the ranch.

To obtain details of the jaguar's private life—its patterns of daily movement, frequency of killing, and kinds of social contact—I needed to use radiotelemetry. Catching a jaguar and collaring it with a radio transmitter should be easy, I reasoned. I would need only to hang meat near the trail and conceal around it several foot snares to hold the cat securely and safely, just as they trap bears and pumas in the United States. The snare design is simple: an animal depresses the hidden trigger, releasing a spring that flips up and tightens a cable around the cat's foot.

But the jaguars were disinterested in my baits, live or dead. In the morning I would find tracks heading straight toward the trap site, but they continued past without even breaking stride. I tried to entice the cats with scents, such as that of another jaguar's feces, and to arouse their curiosity with a caged bird—all to no avail. Then, resorting to another technique, I eliminated the meat baits and carefully concealed snares directly on the trails. Jaguars now stepped into the traps but reacted so swiftly on sensing danger that the snares failed to catch them. On the other hand, the snares worked too well on cattle, and liberating a furious seven-hundred-pound cow provided some interesting moments.

Not only did the jaguars elude me, they actually seemed to taunt my efforts: a female ambled past our hammocks as we slept, and a male deposited his kill—an uneaten capybara—three hundred feet from camp. Though exasperated, I admired the jaguar's ability to outwit me. With its blunt, broad head and powerful shoulders, the cat gives an impression more of archaic brawn than of astuteness, and I had carelessly underrated it.

Since my attempts to snare a jaguar had failed, I turned to the traditional Brazilian methods of hunting the cats. In one, a hunter floats silently in a boat near shore at night, periodically grunting into a hollow gourd to produce a loud, resonant sound much like a jaguar's roar. Attracted by the call, the animal meets not a compatriot but the startling beam of a flashlight followed by the searing stab of a bullet. The other method is to harass a cat with dogs until it either climbs a tree or stands at bay in a thicket, where it can then be shot or, in line with my interests, tranquilized.

Richard Mason, an expatriate Britisher, owns the best pack of hunting dogs in western Brazil, where he took foreign clients on hunting trips until a 1967 federal law protecting jaguars affected his business. He agreed to help me and arrived at Acurizal with five dogs and his tracker, Manuel Dantas, who as hunter and guide had spent twenty-five years in the Pantanal.

The lead dog, Gigante, a castrated yellow mongrel, roamed ahead, quartering the forest in search of fresh jaguar spoor. The other dogs strained and whimpered on their leashes as we followed Gigante's occasional yip. Dantas went first, cutting a trail with short strokes of his machete. "Hup, brriii," Richard called at intervals, urging Gigante on and letting him know that we were still with him.

For hours, and then for days, we crisscrossed the jaguars' haunts without finding any recent tracks. During the months prior to the hunt, I had spent a great deal of time on the Bela Vista ranch just to the north of Acurizal. Had the jaguars moved away in that interval? I doubted it. Where then were the mother and her daughter?

One day we were in Acurizal's most remote area, a somber, wooded gorge. Gigante was ahead—his barks telling us that he was interested in, but not unduly excited by, some scent trail—while we loitered in the dry bed of a mountain stream, uncertain of where to search next. Suddenly Gigante yelped repeatedly, as if being beaten. Then, silence.

"That dog is being hurt! Maybe he found peccaries, or maybe a cat," cried Dantas. We released the clamoring hounds, and they bolted up the valley. Soon their barks fused into a continuous uproar, with only the booming call of Bagunsa, the Troublemaker, still clearly distinguishable.

We hurried after the dogs, crashing through palm thickets and plunging over deadfalls to where they crowded around a tree inclined over a streambed. Seething with excitement, the dogs leaped against the trunk and bit at the lianas hanging from it. Lying on a branch twenty-five feet above the chaos was a jaguar, a young female, strangely calm as she gazed expressionlessly at us and the frenzied dogs. "Finally we meet," I said to myself. While I loaded a syringe with a sleep-inducing drug, Dantas removed the dogs and tied them to a tree a few hundred feet away.

70

As soon as the syringe hit the cat's thigh we retreated to await the effects of the drug. She then clambered down the trunk and vanished into the undergrowth. Ten minutes later we tracked her with a dog, finding her asleep three hundred feet away.

To reward Gigante for his excellent work, we led him to the cat. Even though her agate claws had only minutes earlier sliced into his body, he looked at her quiet form without expression. We did not know then that this was the dog's last hunt, that his life's blood was slowly draining away within him.

"In other hunts the cat would be dead long ago. I would be skinning it now," commented Dantas as we prepared to record her vital statistics. She tipped the scales at 133 pounds and measured sixty-six inches from tip of nose to tip of tail—a small animal by Pantanal standards, where jaguars grow larger than anywhere else in South America. Richard, who carefully weighs trophies, told me that the average adult female is about 165 pounds and that his heaviest male reached 262 pounds. Peter and I then attached the radio collar.

An hour and a quarter after being tranquilized, the jaguar stumbled off, still unsteady on her feet as she angled up a nearby slope. Though pleased by our success, I felt a vague uneasiness that refused to harden into conscious thought. This animal seemed too heavy and her paws too large to be the young Acurizal female I had tracked for months. And where was her mother?

A few days later our cook told us that, according to the gossiping wife of a ranch worker, a jaguar had been killed on Acurizal the previous month. The death of even one animal would seriously disrupt the small population, and we were concerned not only for the animals but also for our project.

Seeking more information, Peter and I went to see Claudio, a ranch hand who had shown great interest in our work, bringing us small animals he had caught and telling us of tracks he had seen. We asked him about the jaguar. As he sat on his mule he looked over our heads toward the dark-edged hills and said, "I don't know anything. I wasn't with the group."

71

We then visited João, a cowhand with the broad, pleasant features of a Bolivian Indian. His eyes slid away from ours when we questioned him. "In some things I have to obey orders," he answered softly and turned away.

Felix, a bushy-bearded squatter, supported a family of twelve by selling manioc, bananas, and other produce. "I know nothing," he said, opening his hands wide in feigned ignorance. "I hunt a few deer and peccary and armadillo. Never jaguars. I tell you all I know."

Unable to break the conspiracy of silence, we proceeded to the hut of Felinho, a cowhand. A pack of mongrels with corrugated ribs hysterically announced our approach. Felinho listened to us and his eyes held no apology as he frankly admitted, "Yes, I shot the jaguar. I have nothing to hide. I didn't tell you about it because you didn't ask." He further related that orders to shoot all jaguars had been given by Geraldo, the absentee manager who checked on the ranch at intervals on behalf of the absentee owner. In Geraldo's opinion, cattle and jaguars cannot coexist. "There is a Brazilian proverb," he once told us. "You can't whistle and chew sugarcane at the same time."

One evening Felinho had surprised the adult female jaguar on a calf kill and shot her with his .22. He sold her skin to a *mascate*, one of the small trading boats plying the Paraguay River. A jaguar skin sells for about 3,000 cruzeiros (equal to about $100); an ocelot, 1,500 cruzeiros; a La Plata otter, 800 cruzeiros; and a caiman, 80 cruzeiros—to name four important trade skins.

In the Pantanal there is legal but no actual protection, and poachers operate with impunity. In San Mauas, just across the Bolivian border, a man named Otis Paraguay has opened a tanning factory to handle the many skins smuggled out of the Pantanal. Alfredo dos Santos and his two sons openly cruise the Paraguay River in a launch from which hunters in dugouts penetrate the swamps and return laden with hides. There are many others whose names are also well known.

The military once apprehended dos Santos with a boatload of skins and turned him over to the civilian authorities. A few days later he was free, all charges dropped. When queried, the official concerned answered, "I don't want to be a dead hero." Frontier law still operates in the sparsely settled Pantanal; piranhas are adept at disposing of dead bodies.

When we pointed out to Felinho that he could be arrested for killing the jaguar, even if ordered by Geraldo, he replied matter-of-factly, "Well, if I go to jail, I'll someday get out and come back. And then I might forget I have children and shoot Geraldo."

One midnight, the cowhand José slipped into the ranch house where we lived. First he asked for rubbing alcohol, which according to local custom is drunk either straight or mixed with milk and sugar. Then he apologized for the late hour, saying that he was afraid to be seen with us, especially by Anibal, the foreman. Anibal has the look of a dyspeptic vulture and a personality to match; all the locals detest him.

Then José informed us that not one but two jaguars had been killed. João, José, and Anibal had discovered the young female—also, like her mother, with a calf kill. Unwilling to abandon the carcass, she tarried and was gunned down. Anibal had cut out her tongue, which when eaten is said to cure rheumatism and other ills, and hidden her skin in his house.

So, as I had suspected, the radio-collared female was new, a subadult animal who apparently had left her place of birth and settled at Acurizal within the past few months. The mother and daughter were dead.

Like Acurizal, many ranches in the area had killed off two or three of their jaguars that year. At Bela Vista, five were shot in 1974. Four years later the population still had not recovered; only four jaguars remained in thirty-six square miles. One hunter shot thirty-seven jaguars on one ranch in a twelve-year period, and another sixty-eight on a different ranch during an eight-year span.

Ranch hands casually kill jaguars, professional hunters guide foreign clients on illegal shoots, and hide collectors take an unknown toll. There are still those today who try to emulate Sasha Siemel, a hunter who with rifle or spear killed more than two hundred jaguars

Anibal, the ranch foreman, holds the hide of a female jaguar who in life was our study animal.

in the Pantanal during the 1920s and 1930s. "It is impossible to kill off all jaguars," one rancher told me smugly. "Some will never be found in the dense bush."

I could have told him that such ignorant words were probably spoken about the passenger pigeon and quagga, too, but I merely stressed that the jaguar is already extinct or reduced to occasional stragglers over large parts of the Pantanal, in some areas because of systematic eradication by ranchers within the past twenty-five years. No species in which a female raises an average of only one cub every two years can stand such heavy attrition. Unless local attitudes change, only a large national park can save the Pantanal jaguar.

The ostensible reason for eliminating jaguars is that they kill cattle. And indeed they do, although the cats account for only a tiny percentage of those that die annually. In one Pantanal district the cattle population declined from about 700,000 to 180,000 in six years, largely as a result of disease, drowning, and starvation, after severe annual floods submerged pastures for months. As a result of poor management on many ranches, only one cow in four or five raises her calf.

While on the Bela Vista ranch, we had radio-collared an adult female jaguar and tracked her for two and a half months, until the radio ceased to function. We made contact with her on thirty-five days. She had preyed on just one calf, a rate of a dozen cattle a year—not a high total, considering that some victims are either feral or would have died of other causes anyway.

This Bela Vista female also revealed interesting facts about jaguar movements. By keeping signal contact with her day and night, we discovered that this supposedly nocturnal animal often wandered through the forest at midday, although she was most active during the hours after dusk and before dawn. She was inactive, probably asleep, for about eight of the twenty-four hours. Her daily travel distances varied from one or two to seven or more miles. Sometimes she remained for several days in a small area, especially if she had a kill. At other times she cruised rapidly, as if by appointment, to some distant place.

I enjoyed tracking this cat at night, alone except for the radio signal that bound me a few hundred feet from her, the forest silent and motionless under a sliver of moon. Listening to the night, examining each shadow for substance, I was filled not only with suspense but also with a quiet feeling of elation.

We radio-tracked the young Acurizal female, too, but did so dutifully, without joy, trying only to gather information on the size of her range. We knew that with the other two jaguars dead we would soon have to seek another study site. Yet this female provided rare hours of pleasure.

Once, shortly past noon, Peter picked up her signal as she traveled along a gallery forest. We followed discreetly, never close enough to glimpse her; only the directional antenna on the receiver indicated her route. She left the shadowy coolness of the forest and plunged into the bright light of rock-bound hills coated sparsely with stunted trees. Steadily she moved on, then suddenly turned back toward us, the signal growing in intensity until Peter whispered, "I can hear her loud without the amplifier."

About three hundred feet away she halted in a fold of the hills and, as we discovered later, reclined near a small pool. There she remained through the fierce heat of day, and she was still there, her signal calm and constant, when the plaintive calls of tinamous (a ground-living bird resembling guinea fowl) announced the coming of night. We stayed on, the jaguar, Peter, and I, together in the darkness. I made myself a bed of dry grass and went to sleep for a while, leaving Peter to listen for the signal at half-hour intervals. Except for brief bouts of activity, the jaguar slept, too, making no effort to hunt. With the first hoarse chorus of howler monkeys at dawn, she moved steadily up the valley, the signal becoming ever fainter until the forests claimed her.

At our request, a forest department official visited Acurizal to investigate the jaguar killings. He also confiscated the jaguar hide that Anibal had secreted in his home. Now, for the first time I met her—the young animal who in life had eluded me. The hide with its sorrowing beauty, its hollow eyes, its bullet hole—I did not want this memory. Was this animal really a part of the past? Among certain Amazonian Indian tribes the jaguar is the representative of the sun, an immortal being that since the dawn of life has been the protector of all that lives, including man, and which upon death climbs back into the sky to begin once again the cosmic circle of rebirth.

[1980]

AFRICA

The survival of our wildlife is a matter of grave concern to all of us in Africa. These wild creatures amid the wild places they inhabit are not only important as a source of wonder and inspiration but are an integral part of our natural resources and of our future livelihood and well-being.

—Julius Kambarage Nyerere,
former president of Tanzania

Thank you, Zebra,
Adorned with your own stripes,
Iridescent and glittering creature,
Whose skin is as soft as girls' is;
One on which the eye dwells all day, as on the
    solitary cow of a poor man;
Creature that makes the forests beautiful.

—Oral poem of the Shona of Zimbabwe,
twentieth century

In the Path of Conflict

Mountain Gorilla

Four decades after I had concluded my gorilla study, I returned to the Virunga Volcanoes in Rwanda with Amy Vedder of the Wildlife Conservation Society to assist a Canadian film team with a documentary. I do not like to return to places where my heart rests, fearful that things have changed: I prefer to keep my old memories. We trudged up the mountain led by guides and protected by armed guards because the forest was not safe from rebels. The guides were superb, diligent and interested, and they knew all seventy gorillas in the four groups by name. Once again I reveled in the presence of these magnificent apes, in their dark beauty, the glint of sun in their calm eyes, the delicate, somewhat sweet smell of the females.

To prevent transmission of disease from human to ape, park visitors are prohibited from going closer than twenty-five feet from a gorilla. But what to do when a gorilla makes contact with you? One day the film crew stood on a narrow trail where the vegetation was flattened by a nearby gorilla group of eleven, led by the silverback male Guhonolo. I was nearby. My field notes describe what happened next: "Something touches my lower leg, a gentle tap as if with the back of the hand. A female gorilla named Gukunda, with an infant on her back, is beside me, trying to get by. 'Oops, sorry,' I say and step aside. She squeezes by. This is the most wonderful wildlife experience I have had. Or rather, it is more than that. It was an honor and compliment to be treated like just another gorilla, as kin. Gukunda touched me."

A recent census found that the number of mountain gorillas in the Virunga Volcanoes region was about 380, reflecting a steady growth in recent years— and a continuing commitment by the Rwandan government to preserve these apes. Soon the population may rebound to about 450, about what it was when I studied the gorillas. I left Rwanda with new and treasured memories.

On January 22, 1991, my wife, Kay, and I sat on the summit of Mount Visoke, one of the eight Virunga Volcanoes that straddle the borders of Rwanda, Zaire [now again called Congo], and Uganda. We had come to help with a mountain gorilla film. That morning we had left the Karisoke Research Center, the base of Dian Fossey's gorilla work from 1967 until she was killed by unknown assailants in 1985. Her hut of green corrugated metal remained, littered with remnants of her past. Still on the wall was a plastic Santa Claus, a poignant reminder that she died at Christmastime. Beside her cabin, shaded by moss-laden boughs of hagenia trees, was her grave, along with those of seventeen gorillas, one dog, and one monkey.

But it was not a day for us to dwell on tragedy. Instead of the swirling gray fog and rain-drenched slopes that are so common here, the volcanoes rose stark and clear above a shimmering forest. To the west, in the saddle between Mikeno and Karisimbi, the two highest volcanoes, was a place called Kabara. Kay and I had lived there in 1959 and 1960 while conducting the first intensive gorilla study. Now, after three decades, we had returned to an idyll of our past.

The gorillas on the slopes of the Virunga Volcanoes—some three hundred animals—inhabit a small forested island surrounded by a sea of people. Twenty miles to the north is Uganda's Impenetrable Forest, now protected as Bwindi Impenetrable National Park, another island with perhaps three hundred gorillas. These 285 square miles represent the entire world of the remaining mountain gorillas. Years ago, when I watched the gorillas' leisurely life, the animals eating and sleeping and

The Virunga Volcanoes straddle the borders of Congo, Rwanda, and Uganda. I did most of my research on mountain gorillas in the Congo during 1959–60. Our base was a hut at a place called Kabara, elevation about 10,000 feet. Porters such as these hauled in the supplies we needed.

tumbling in play, I was glad that they could not fathom their rarity and my concerns. We have a common past, but only humans have been given the mental power to worry about their fate.

Now the radiance of those months returned as intense memories. Once again Kay and I followed a swath of head-high vegetation until soft grumbles signaled contented gorillas ahead. We recalled old gorilla acquaintances: Big Daddy, the silverback leader of a large group, his power majestic even in repose, and Junior, a reckless young male that liked to linger near us. Once a female with an infant on her back had climbed with startling innocence upon a low branch to sit with me, probably the first time that a wild gorilla and a human were amicably side by side.

However, to me that gorilla study had meaning beyond the gathering of new facts. Gorillas had long been viewed as symbols of savagery, "exceedingly ferocious" in temper, as a nineteenth-century missionary phrased it. My task was not to capture or master them but solely to interpret their life. So I approached them with empathy and respect, wanting nothing from them but peace and proximity. And they accepted my presence with an astounding generosity of spirit. The recent decades have been a turning point, indeed a revolution, in our relationship with animals. Humans have begun to overcome cross-species barriers, achieving intimacy with humpback whales, chimpanzees, lions, mountain sheep, wolves. The gorillas of popular image were a fantasy. It pleases me that I helped change perceptions.

The gorilla, of course, is more than an animal. These apes are a primal part of human heritage. Our kin. We traveled down different evolutionary paths, the gorillas creating their own world, complete and coherent, and humans shaping theirs. No one who looks into a gorilla's eyes—intelligent, gentle, vulnerable—can remain unchanged, for the gap between ape and human vanishes; we know that the gorilla still lives within us. Do gorillas also recognize this ancient connection?

Our reveries that day on Mount Visoke were shattered by a walkie-talkie message from the lowlands: the Rwandan Patriotic Front—led by ethnic Tutsi—had invaded from Uganda. We were ordered to leave the mountains immediately. Led by primatologist Diane Doran, the director of Karisoke at the time, we descended to the town of Ruhengeri. Caught in the middle of a battle between rebels and the Rwandan Army the following day, we were evacuated by French paratroopers.

Ironically, Kay and I also had to terminate our 1960 project because of war. The then–Belgian Congo gained independence that year, and with it came years of unrest. And in Rwanda, a Belgian protectorate until 1962, the Hutu tribe waged a civil war against the ruling Tutsi. Many Tutsi fled the country, living in exile until they invaded their former homeland in 1990. The renewed war climaxed in the carnage of

A subadult male mountain gorilla peels a stalk of wild celery, one of the gorilla's favorite foods. This photo was taken in 2001, when I returned to the Virungas to help with a documentary.

April 1994; soon after, the Rwandan Patriotic Front achieved victory and formed a new government.

The mountain gorillas have a long past but only a century of history, much of it turbulent. This history began in 1902, when a German officer, Capt. Oscar von Beringe, first encountered the apes—and shot two. In the next quarter century, collectors and hunters captured or killed more than fifty gorillas in the Virunga region. Carl Akeley of the

American Museum of Natural History shot five gorillas in 1921, but he was so impressed with the apes that he prompted the Belgian government to establish Africa's first national park, Albert National Park, for them in 1925.

Belgian protection gave the gorillas relative peace until the turmoil in 1960, when the Belgian park staff fled. Civil war, insurrection, and the division of Albert Park into Congolese and Rwandan sectors demoralized the guard force. Cattle invaded the fragile uplands, and poachers roamed the forests. Their wire snares cut deep into the gorillas' flesh, but some managed to tear free. In one group of eleven gorillas two animals had only one hand each; another's hand was deformed. Gorilla hands and heads were sold as souvenirs to tourists. And the gorillas lost much forest. In 1958 the Belgians in Rwanda turned over twenty-seven square miles of gorilla habitat to farmers, and in 1968 another thirty-eight square miles, or 40 percent of the remaining forest, was given to a European-sponsored agricultural scheme. It was a desolate time, to which the gorillas could be only mute and passive witnesses.

Gorilla numbers plummeted. In 1960 I estimated about 450 in the Virunga region. Censuses during the 1970s showed around 275, and by 1981 there were only 250. During this critical time Dian Fossey, assisted for varying periods by Craig Sholley, David Watts, Kelly Stewart, Ian Redmond, Alexander Harcourt, and others, was at Karisoke. Dian harassed poachers with obsessive zeal. And she made the world aware of the gorillas' plight. Her heroic vigil helped the apes endure. However, her unyielding confrontational approach with local people, which she termed "expedient action," ultimately cannot save wildlife. Conservation depends on the goodwill of the local population.

A new era in gorilla conservation began in 1978, when Amy Vedder and Bill Weber of the Wildlife Conservation Society in New York arrived to establish gorilla tourism and an education program for the Rwandans. The following year their work was incorporated into the Mountain Gorilla Project, financed by an international consortium of conservation organizations. This integrated program of antipoaching, tourism, and education, all in cooperation with a receptive Rwandan government, had a marked impact on local attitudes.

A well-trained guard force maintained the national park. The education program created widespread awareness not just of the gorillas but also of the need to protect forests. The Virungas in Rwanda represent less than half of 1 percent of the country's land area but 10 percent of its water catchment. Without the forests to store water, streams would disappear during the dry season and deprive the dense human population of water. Four gorilla groups were soon habituated to tourists viewing them at close range. Fees for tourists were high, yet so enthralled were visitors that gorilla viewing became at one time Rwanda's third-largest earner of foreign exchange. Similar programs were later initiated on the Congo and Uganda sides of the volcanoes.

The Mountain Gorilla Project also had an unforeseen impact: the people of Rwanda became proud of their apes. The gorillas became part of Rwanda's identity in the world, part of the nation's vision of itself.

The 1980s were a golden time for the thirty or so gorilla groups on the Virunga Volcanoes, and the population grew again, to about 320. The innovative program initiated by Amy Vedder and Bill Weber had become a classic story of conservation success, one whose approach has been emulated many times. Then the most recent civil war violated the gorillas' peaceful existence once again. Yet in spite of the turmoil, with soldiers of both factions traversing the forests, the gorillas have not been decimated. Indeed the Rwandan Patriotic Front expressed public concern for the gorillas' safety even while it was fighting. The new prime minister, Faustin Twagiramungu, has affirmed his country's commitment to the apes.

Given the urgent and crushing social needs of Rwanda, this declaration is remarkable. For one species to fight for the survival of another, even in times of stress, is something new in evolution. In this, more than all our technology, lies our claim to being human.

[1995]

❧

Author's note: *The following excerpt from* The Year of the Gorilla *describes a day in September 1959, some six months into my study of mountain gorillas in the Virunga Volcanoes. Our home base for more than a year was a rough wooden hut at Kabara, at 10,200 feet in the saddle between Mount Karisimbi and Mount Mikeno, on the Congolese side of the volcanoes. From there Kay and I went in search of gorillas to observe them. Several different bands of gorillas were identified during the study; I observed members of group IV more than any others.*

Kay prepares our simple dinner, usually a one-pot meal such as rice with tinned meat.

I write up notes while huddled by our small woodstove in the Kabara hut. PHOTO BY KAY SCHALLER.

On the last day of August, as N'sekanabo and I clambered up the boulder-strewn depths of Kanyamagufa Canyon, a tremendous roar filled the chasm and, bounding from wall to wall, descended the mountain like the rumbling of an avalanche. We started and ducked and then peered up at the silverback male who, surrounded by his group, stood motionless at the canyon rim looking down at us. Quietly and as unobtrusively as possible we retraced our steps under the watchful eye of the male, feeling chastised like children for having so crassly intruded into his domain. . . .

Almost daily throughout the month of September I visited these animals, group IV, watching them, enjoying their antics, and worrying over their problems. All the members in the group became definite individuals whom I recognized and named. No other group taught me as much or took a greater hold on my affection.

They moved up the precipitous slopes of Mount Mikeno after our first meeting, going higher and higher until the *Hypericum* trees grew stunted and the timberline was not far above. I ascended the mountain daily to be with the animals, my senses vibrant and alive as I clambered up. The silent forests were another world from the villages and fields that lay far below us. On the horizon, past Goma and Lake Kivu, dense ranks of clouds gathered, as they usually did by mid-morning, drawing closer and closer until their advance was halted by the ramparts of the mountains. But drawn inexorably onward they stormed soundlessly up the slopes, fingering the canyons, dodging from tree to tree, until finally they had gathered everything into their clammy embrace.

On September 4, I came upon the gorillas feeding slowly on a steep slope about a hundred yards above me. I sat down at the base of a tree, and with binoculars resting on my drawn-up knees, I scanned the slope, trying to pinpoint the whereabouts of the four silverback males in the group. The large male gorillas are the most alert, unpredictable, and excitable members of the group and hence the most dangerous. Squatting with his back toward me was Big Daddy, easily recognizable by the two bright silver spots on his gray back. As he turned to rest on his belly, he saw me, gave me an intent look, and emitted two sharp grunts. Several females and youngsters glanced from the vegetation in his direction and then ambled to his side, warned that possible danger was near. Big Daddy was the undisputed leader of the group, a benign dictator who by his actions determined the behavior of the other animals. Now he stood looking down at me with slightly parted lips, his mighty arms propped on a knoll, completely certain of his status and his power, a picture of sublime dignity.

D.J. was the striving executive type who had not yet reached the top. He was second in command, a rather frustrating position from a human point of view, for in such matters as determining the direction of travel and the time and duration of rest periods, the females and youngsters ignored him completely. He lay by himself on his back, one arm slung casually across his face, oblivious to the world.

The Outsider roamed slowly around the periphery of the group, intent on his own doings. He was a gigantic male in the prime of life, visibly larger than Big Daddy, and by far the heaviest male around Kabara. His nostrils were set like two black coals in his face, and his expression conveyed an independence of spirit and a glowering temper. His gait was somewhat rolling, like that of a seaman, and with each step his paunch swayed back and forth. To estimate accurately the weight of gorillas in the wild is difficult, but I believe that the Outsider must have weighed between 450 and 480 pounds. Gorilla males are often said to weigh 600 pounds or more, but these are the weights of obese zoo animals. Two mountain gorillas in the San Diego Zoo, for example, weighed that much, and they gained still more before they died. In contrast, of ten adult male mountain gorillas killed and weighed in the wild by hunters and collectors, the heaviest animal reached 482 pounds, and the average was about 375 pounds.

The fourth silverback male in the group was Splitnose, so named for the ragged cut that divided the upper part of his left nostril. He was young, his back barely turned silver, and he lacked the quiet reserve, the sureness of action, that characterized the other three adult males. As if to compensate for his uncertainty, he was highly vociferous whenever he saw me, roaring again and again, sounding his warning over the mountains. But none of the other animals responded visibly.

Apparently D.J. had hatched a plan, for suddenly he left his resting place and circled uphill. Then stealthily, very stealthily, he angled toward me, keeping behind a screen of shrubs. But gorillas are not very good at this sort of thing. Branches broke underfoot and to orient himself he stood up to glance over the vegetation. As soon as I looked directly at him, he ducked and sat quietly before continuing his stalk. He advanced to within thirty feet of me before emitting a terrific roar and beating his chest. Immediately afterward, before the echo of the sound had died away, he peered out from between the bushes as if to see how I had responded to his commotion. Never, even when I fully expected it, was I able to get used to the roar of a silverback male. The suddenness of the

A subadult male we named the Kicker beats his chest in agitation when he sees me quietly watching nearby. The females and youngsters stoically look on.

sound, the shattering volume, invariably made me want to run. But I derived immense satisfaction from noting that the other gorillas in the group startled at a roar just as visibly as I did.

With the male only thirty feet from me, I became uneasy and thought it prudent to retreat to a safer place. Cautiously, I ascended a tree to a height of ten feet. One of the ten females in the group left Big Daddy and ambled to within seventy feet of me to sit on a stump, her chin propped on her folded arms. Slowly, as if daring each other to move closer, the whole group advanced toward my tree. I felt a brief spasm of panic, for the gorillas had never behaved in this manner before. They congregated behind some bushes, and three females carrying infants and two juveniles ascended a tree and tried to obtain a better view of me through the interlacing vines that festooned the branches. In the ensuing minutes we played a game of peek-a-boo: whenever I craned my neck to see the gorillas more clearly, they ducked their heads, only to pop forth again as soon as I looked away. One juvenile, perhaps four years old, climbed into a small tree adjacent to mine, and there we sat, fifteen feet apart, each somewhat nervously glancing at the other, both of us curious, but refraining from staring directly to eliminate all intimation of threat.

Junior, the only blackbacked male in the group, stepped out from behind the shrubbery and advanced to within ten feet of the base of my tree, biting off and eating a tender leaf from a blackberry bush on the way. He stood on all fours and looked up at me, mouth slightly open. In all my hours with group IV, I was never able to fathom Junior completely. He was less than eight years old, still the size of a female, but his body had already taken on the angular and muscular build of a male. There was recklessness in his face and a natural mischievousness, which even his inherent reserve could not hide. At the same time his look conveyed a critical aloofness, as if he were taking my measure and was not quite sure if I could be fully trusted. He was the only gorilla who seemed to derive any sort of satisfaction from being near me. Later in the month, rarely a day went by when he did not leave the group to sit by me, either quietly watching my every action or sleeping with his back toward me. Today he was still somewhat uncertain of himself, as his indrawn and compressed lips showed. Man too bites his lips when nervous. Occasionally he slapped the ground with a wild overhand swipe, using the palm of his hand, then slyly looked up at me, apparently with the hope that his wanton gesture had been startling. The other members of the group rested quietly. Every fifteen or twenty minutes one of the males jerked out of his slumber to roar once or twice before reclining again to continue his nap.

All apprehension of the gorillas had long since left me. Not once had their actions portrayed ferocity or even outright anger. The silverback males were somewhat annoyed, to be sure, and several animals were excited, but all this was offset by their curiosity concerning me and their rapid acceptance of me. As long as I remained quiet, they felt so safe that they continued their daily routine even to the extent of taking their naps beside the tree in which I was sitting. Early in the study I had noted that the gorillas tend to have an extremely placid nature which is not easily aroused to excitement. They give the impression of being stoic and reserved, of being introverted. Their expression is usually one of repose, even in situations that to me would have been disturbing. All their emotions are in their eyes, which are a soft, dark brown. The eyes have a language of their own, being subtle and silent mirrors of the mind, revealing constantly changing patterns of emotion that in no other visible way affect the expression of the animal. I could see hesitation and uneasiness, curiosity and boldness and annoyance. Sometimes, when I met a gorilla face to face, the expression in its eyes more than anything else told me of his feelings and helped me decide my course of action.

The brief morning spell of sunshine had given way to dank clouds that descended to the level of the trees. For five hours I perched on a branch, chilled through and through, my fingers so stiff I was barely able to take notes. It began to rain heavily, and soon the rain turned to hail. The gorillas sat in a hunched position, letting the marble-sized stones bounce off their backs. They looked thoroughly miserable with the water dripping off their brow ridges, and the long hairs on their arms were a sodden mass. I sat huddled next to the trunk of the tree, hoping for some protection from the canopy. My face was close to the bark, and I smelled the fungus-like odor of lichen and moldy moss. I could not leave the gorillas without disturbing them, and I had to wait until they moved away.

After the hail ceased and the rain was a mere drizzle, the gorillas spread out to forage. From behind a bush came a curious staccato sound, which I had not heard before: a rapid series of loud *ö—ö-ö-ö*, with the first vowel forceful, emphatic, and separated from the others by a distinct pause. This sound was emitted over and over again, and after two or three minutes I became aware of the situation that elicited it. D.J. and a female were together. They were copulating. She rested on her knees, belly, and elbows, and D.J. was mounted behind, holding onto her hips. The male pushed, and since the slope was steep, the two animals moved downhill. They covered forty feet in fifteen minutes, with the female using her hands to part vegetation as they progressed. They stopped three times. D.J. was thrusting rapidly.

His vocalizations grew harsher, and the female screamed piercingly. The male now clasped her by the armpits, and he was nearly covering her back. They came to rest against a tree trunk, and a hoarse, trembling sound, almost a roar, escaped from D.J.'s parted lips, interrupted by sharp intakes of breath. He sat back, the act completed. The female lay motionless for ten seconds, then walked slowly uphill, while the male remained, panting. In spite of these far from silent doings, none of the other members of the group paid the slightest attention. Even Big Daddy, the boss, who rested in full view of the copulators, was seemingly oblivious of the spectacle.

At last the gorillas moved away and, after six hours on the branch, I was able to descend, stiff and cold. In spite of the inclement weather, I was elated by the perfection of the day.

[1964]

Memories of Eden

Serengeti

After many years, I returned to the Serengeti in 1996 with a tour group from the Wildlife Conservation Society. I was also on a personal pilgrimage. Seeing once more the migrating zebras outlined against black storm clouds, and the landscape of graceful umbrella acacias with its indolent lion prides, I was struck by the timeless quality of the landscape. But I also knew that changes were occurring ever more rapidly, with an increasing onslaught of people.

During the twentieth century the ecosystem lost 40 percent of its land to pastoralists and agriculturalists. About 1.7 million people now live along just the western edge of the park, where they encroach on the land and kill thousands of wildebeest, buffalo, impala, and others every year for food and market. Moral exhortations without tangible economic incentives will not halt such attrition. Village involvement in the park and its wildlife has become essential. Income from community-based tourism and from sport hunters in concessions near the park, for example, could provide health, education, and other services, and limited subsistence hunting by traditional methods under a village quota system might even be considered outside the park. Whatever the solutions, we all have an obligation to ensure that the Serengeti—one of the world's great natural wonders—remains part of our heritage.

For over three years during the late 1960s, Kay, our two small sons, and I made our home in the Serengeti National Park. We lived in a wooden

Our family spent the years from 1966 to 1969 in the Serengeti, where all the photos in the next few chapters were taken. Our home at Seronera, the Serengeti park headquarters, was a bungalow shaded by acacia trees on which giraffes came to browse.

bungalow shaded by flat-topped acacias, where plains gave way to woodlands at a place called Seronera. Daily I roamed in search of lions, whose life I had come to study. At the beginning of the dry season in May, when grass on the plains becomes dry stubble and the sky is cloudless and pale, as if seen through a luminous gauze, much of the wildlife retreats to the woodlands, where grass and water are plentiful. Wildebeest and zebras flow westward, a throbbing stream of life drawn by a collective will, the animals trudging in long lines, often several abreast. They follow their age-old migration west and then north, many moving out of Tanzania into Kenya's Masai Mara Game Reserve.

I liked the woodlands in spite of persistent tsetse flies. Lemon-barked fever trees line stream banks, and borassus palms are there, too, in primitive elegance. Herds of skittish impala come to drink at pools, elephants move like floating gray boulders through the thickets, and flocks of Fisher's lovebirds pass overhead, handfuls of emeralds tossed into the sky. When in November or December black pillars of rain announce a change of season, the migratory animals return to the plains to feast on nutrient-rich grass. It pleased me to follow this vagrant wandering—I liked the plains best.

Nomadic lions trailed the great herds too, and resident prides at the edge of the woodlands shifted into the open. I watched them in daytime, the animals conveying indolent power even when in repose. I followed them also on hunts at night, the plains suffused with the moon's silver light. The thunder of fleeing herds shattered the silence, sometimes punctuated by the dying scream of a zebra. The cats bolted down the meat, snarling and snapping, their emotions so naked that the scene filled me with primal fear even in the safety of a Land Rover. The air was heavy with the odor of blood and rumen content.

Sometimes, however, I abandoned this scientific quest to venture onto plains where there were no roads, no people, nothing to violate the peace; where there were only animals and the green curve of a horizon broken by wind-worn outcrops of stone called kopjes. There wildebeest croaked like gigantic frogs, Thompson's gazelles twitched their tails, and vultures soared stiff-winged overhead. It was a scene of pastoral delight, an eternal beginning where animals lived unaffected by today's complexities. I left my vehicle behind and, deprived of this armor, strode across the sea of grass, a lone figure free to roam, intoxicated by the wild beauty and vastness, which humankind has not yet shaped to its will. I climbed a kopje, eyed by blue-and-red agama lizards, and reclined on the warm rock, exposed to, yet converging with, the environment.

Below, in brilliant light, heat waves danced like a choppy sea before the wind and distorted wildebeest, zebras, eland, and others into phantom creatures. Ancient connections seemingly at the edge of memory crowded the mind, and dreams of resurrecting the past were almost palpable. Over a million years ago this landscape with its acacia woodlands, plains, and lakes was much as it is today, but the fauna was much more diverse, a biologist's delight. Around and on my kopje roamed various

Our family enjoyed picnics on the kopjes, large granite outcrops on the Serengeti plains, also a favorite resting place of lions and leopards.

species now extinct for reasons unknown. Chalicotheres, related to horses and tapirs, moved by ponderously; a giraffe with palmate horns, *Libytherium*, browsed on trees; *Simopithecus*, gorilla-sized baboons, scampered over the kopje; *Afrochoerus*, a long-tusked pig as large as a rhinoceros, rooted in nearby swamps; and saber-toothed cats prowled the shadows. To the east, near the base of the highlands, lies Olduvai Gorge, where humankind had its roots, a vanished legacy of various hominids. They, too, sat on this kopje. But unlike them, I bore witness to the last days of Eden, the last great gathering of herds; I saw no more than a fragile illusion of the Pleistocene.

Since the 1950s many biologists have worked in the Serengeti ecosystem, an area of 10,000 square miles. The Serengeti Research Institute was established in 1966 and continues under the name Serengeti Wildlife Research Center. Research on animals, vegetation, climate, soils, and other topics has contributed to an understanding of how the ecosystem works. In 1957, Bernhard and Michael Grzimek were pioneers whose book *Serengeti Shall Not Die* focused the world's consciousness on that priceless heritage hidden in Tanzania. A. R. E. Sinclair devoted over two decades to monitoring populations of wildebeest, buffalo, and other species, and Sam McNaughton studied the interactions between grasses and herbivores for many years; their long-term efforts have made important contributions to protecting and managing the Serengeti. In the Ngorongoro Conservation Unit adjoining the Serengeti, Patricia Moehlman trained teams of Tanzanians in ecological monitoring techniques. This essential task had too long been neglected by expatriate researchers, even though the future of the Serengeti depends on the initiative, dedication, and knowledge of Tanzanians.

Written records of the Serengeti date back only to the turn of the century. Yet even this brief span serves as a reminder that the Serengeti as we know it is but a fragile moment in time, that no ecosystem remains static. Rinderpest, a viral disease whose natural host is cattle, struck East Africa in 1890, and within two years about 95 percent of the wildebeest and buffalo had died. Deprived of life-sustaining livestock, many members of the Masai and other tribes perished in famine; deprived of wildlife, some lions became man-eaters. People retreated from the Serengeti region, their departure reducing woodland fires that had kept growth in check by killing seedlings. Grass glades now converted to thickets. Veterinary treatment of livestock eliminated the disease in cattle, and by the early 1960s it had disappeared in wildlife as well. Wildebeest and buffalo now increased rapidly in number. Wildebeest rose from 250,000 in 1961 to 500,000 in 1967, and buffalo from 30,000 to 50,000 during the same period, whereas zebras, not affected by the disease, remained stable in number.

A new factor began to have an impact on wildlife in 1971. Lack of rainfall during the dry season had limited the grass supply of herbivores, keeping populations in check, but suddenly more frequent and widespread showers enabled some populations to expand to new limits.

I rescued an abandoned and starving lion cub, which taught me many things about lion behavior and was a feisty companion to my sons. Ramses, shown here with my son Mark, ultimately went to the Milwaukee Zoo, where he fathered many cubs.

Wildebeest reached 1.3 million by 1977, then leveled off; buffalo increased to 75,000, and topi also became more abundant. As settlers arrived in ever larger numbers around the periphery of the park, fires progressively turned woodland to grassland. But now, with so many wildebeest eating and trampling the tall grass, the incidence of fire declined, allowing the trees to regenerate. The country again became more bushy, as in the early part of the twentieth century, benefiting browsers such as the giraffe.

Today, with more grass available on the plains during the dry season, gazelles, zebras, and others remain there in greater numbers, which, in turn, has enabled hyenas to increase. New lion prides have established themselves where none could exist before, and those already present have increased in size. A climatic change back to the drier period may well cause the wildebeest population to crash, and once more initiate far-reaching changes in the ecosystem.

Poachers also have an impact on wildlife. In the mid-1970s lack of funds almost halted antipoaching efforts for a decade. Buffalo were reduced by more than 50 percent and elephants, which greatly affect woodlands by pushing over mature trees, by 85 percent, reducing the herd to a mere 350 animals.

The web of life is intricate, the relationships complex. Much of the research in the Serengeti has a significant application when making decisions about the ecosystem's future. At present the integrity of the park is threatened by encroaching agriculturalists, poachers, a railroad, and cattle ranches. And someone has actually proposed that "the Serengeti migration could produce perhaps forty million tins of canned meat each year without any decline in the total wildebeest, zebra, and gazelle numbers." Other considerations aside, cropping wildlife would promote instability in the ecosystem, upsetting the dynamic balance between herbivores and their food supply and between predator and prey. And it would negate three decades of research on the natural regulation of animal numbers.

Forty million tins of canned meat. Preservation for profit should not be the ultimate goal. Tanzania has maintained the Serengeti in spite of crushing social needs not for economic reasons but as a statement of the nation's vision and identity. The Serengeti does, however, have inestimable value as a genetic storehouse of numerous species. At some future date, when we are ready to mend and restore what has been squandered, the grasses and animals may provide stock for rehabilitating other pastures. Parks such as the Serengeti also provide valuable natural laboratories, baselines against which changes elsewhere can be measured and placed into perspective. But, above all, certain places are so unique in the pleasure and inspiration they afford that they must be preserved without compromise as repositories of beauty—as living museums. They must remain unmanaged, as original fragments of our past. Unaffected by human greed, their survival will be witness to man's moral obligation to society and to other species. And there must be a global commitment to maintain such cultural resources. As Edward

Hoagland phrased it in another context, the Serengeti should be viewed as "the best and final future place to make a leisurely traverse or enjoy a camping trip that [is] not rooted in our century."

Yearning for hope and thriving on dreams, we find what we seek in the Serengeti. At least once in a lifetime every person should make a pilgrimage into the wilderness to dwell on its wonders and discover the idyll of a past now largely gone. If I had to select just one such spot on Earth, it would be the Serengeti. There dwell the fierce ghosts of our human past; there animals seek their destiny, living monuments to a time when we were still wanderers on a prehistoric Earth. To witness that calm rhythm of life revives our worn souls and recaptures a feeling of belonging to the natural world. No one can return from the Serengeti unchanged, for tawny lions will forever prowl our memory and great herds throng our imagination.

[1989]

Watching the Pride

Lion

W hen *my family and I left the Serengeti in 1969 after three years, it was with a feeling of loss. We had become acquainted with many lions and been aware of their joys and problems. Later I wrote that "knowing such animals individually, one begins to view an area with a new intimacy and with a caring that turns into a special enchantment; and then, as life renews itself, there is a feeling that things will continue unchanged for ever and ever." Fortunately my research was continued by a succession of other biologists, and the work still produces fascinating new insights after forty years. I learned, for example, what happened to each member of my two main prides, when new males evicted the old ones, when the female Flop-ear died (at about fifteen years of age), and when in 1979 the last of the original females died, at about sixteen years old. These lions are gone, but their lineages continue.*

Since 1978, Craig Packer of the University of Minnesota and his coworkers have monitored the lions and elucidated aspects of lion society that I could only describe in general terms. The new technology of molecular genetics, of DNA fingerprinting, has demonstrated conclusively that pride females are closely related, whereas adult males—whose pride tenure is short—may be related or unrelated. The importance of long-term studies was confirmed in 1994 when about a third of the Serengeti lions, some thousand animals, died of the canine distemper virus, acquired from the many village dogs just outside the park boundary. By 1999 the population had recovered.

However, the lion is in trouble throughout Africa, killed when it preys on livestock (as well as occasionally on people) and evicted from ever-shrinking habitat. Only about thirty thousand lions survive, over a quarter of them in Tanzania. The lion has captured our imagination like few other creatures, so much so that tourists on visits to Africa mainly want to see the cat or even just hear the male's thundering roar. Deafening silence will fill the African night unless everyone looks upon the lion with greater compassion.

In the sparse shade of an acacia tree, the members of a lion pride rested. I had visited these animals almost daily since beginning a three-year study of lions, and I had given many of them names. Flop-ear tenderly cleaned one of her cubs with long strokes of her tongue while another lioness, called Notch because of a tear in her ear, lay sprawled motionless except when flicking her tail to keep off flies. A cub thought that the lively black tassel at the end of Notch's tail was designed solely for its amusement, and it pawed, pounced on, and shook it with playful abandon. Asleep, too, was the Old One, the pride matriarch whose canines were worn to mere stumps; near her, in noble repose, were Black Mane and Brown Mane, two of the pride males. These, and others, rested with legs and bodies touching, a contented, tawny mass in the middle of Tanzania's Serengeti Plain.

It was an idyllic vision of Africa distilled to its essence, and at that moment the popular image of lion society seemed touchingly true: the lioness as the epitome of the good mother, the male lazy and lordly, waiting to snatch the lion's share of any kill, and the cubs secure in a loving pride, with little to do but sleep and play. An incident occurred not long after I began my research, however, that put the pride in an altogether different perspective.

As I watched one night in the light of a pale moon, several of the lionesses caught a zebra. Filling the night with menacing snarls, the lions fought over their meal, the air heavy with the odor of blood.

A lioness and cub at a zebra carcass. Cubs may not be allowed to feed at a kill until adult members of the pride are sated.

The carcass was soon dismembered, but not until Flop-ear and Notch finished their meal did they amble off to fetch the cubs they had cached some distance away. When the hungry cubs reached the kill site, they found not a communal feast but a group of solitary diners, each jealously guarding its portion of zebra. No lioness, even though gorged, would share her meat. Agate claws sliced past the face of any cub that dared ignore a lioness's sinister growls of warning. However, Brown Mane had the head and neck of the zebra in his possession and, unlike the lionesses, he generously permitted the cubs to dine with him.

Could it be, I wondered, that a lioness is actually a poor mother and that the male is more than just a parasite on the pride? A pride, I learned, is a complex society in which each member plays a subtle role. And, as in any society, its young must learn the rules of social life. They must learn what they may and may not do—or perish. It intrigued me how cubs accomplished this, for the lion is a unique cat, the only truly social cat in existence.

The highly social lions of the Serengeti enjoy physical contact and many forms of play.

Whereas a typical cat mother raises her offspring alone, avoiding contact with others of her kind, a lioness lives with her relatives, her sisters, mother, grandmother, and various aunts. All lionesses in a pride are related and remain together for life. Unrelated females are hardly ever accepted. A pride also contains one to five adult males, but unlike the lionesses they are not permanent members. After few months or years, a stronger rival may oust them, appropriating the lionesses and also the territory it which these live. Evicted males become nomads, wanderers in search of another pride to claim as their own.

Lion cubs begin life, as do other cats, in contact with only their mother and two to three siblings. After a gestation period of three and a half months, the cubs are born in a thicket or other hiding place. Weighing a mere three pounds and barely able to crawl, newborn lions are helpless. Their eyes open three to fifteen days after birth, blue-gray eyes that slowly over months turn golden. At three weeks, the first teeth erupt, and the cubs take their first unsteady steps. Still, they remain in seclusion, usually waiting quietly for their mother to return.

It didn't take me long to discover that, by human standards, lionesses often are surprisingly inept mothers. For instance, Lioness A, as I labeled her in my notes, was elderly and through long experience presumably a competent mother. One night she killed a wildebeest, and for obscure reasons she then carried one of her cubs, only a week old and unable to eat meat, to the carcass. In her absence, a leopard found the kill and enjoyed a free meal. Seeing the lioness return, the leopard retreated into a nearby tree. After placing her cub beside the wildebeest, the lioness was in an awkward position: she wanted to fetch her other cub yet guard the first one from the leopard. What to do?

After some indecision, she departed for the other cub, leaving the first one behind, and the leopard promptly killed it. On her return, Lioness A rested throughout that day and the following night beside her two cubs, one alive and one dead. While on a dawn patrol of their territory, Black Mane and Brown Mane discovered and joined the family. Carelessly they flopped down, accidentally squashing the remaining cub. Luckily, nature takes such deaths into account. A lioness can have another litter within four months.

In describing lion life, it's tempting to dwell on the dramatic at the expense of the mundane. Most cubs that die are not deliberately killed but vanish quietly, no doubt abandoned by their mothers. Lionesses often stay away from their cubs for twenty-four hours or more. Sometimes they are hunting; at other times they prefer the conviviality of the pride to an isolated lair. Being self-indulgent, some lionesses may simply not bother to return to suckle their cubs.

If neglect were not tempered by devotion, of course, few cubs would survive. Lion-watching offers no greater delight than to witness cubs who, having waited silently apprehensive all day, finally see their mother return. Exuberantly they greet her, bounding playfully against her and rubbing their bodies along her flanks in an orgy of affection. As she flops down, the youngsters start to nurse, meowing harshly in a frenzy to relieve their hunger.

When cubs are about six weeks old, they are strong enough to follow their mother and also able to add meat to their diet of milk. At that age, a lioness may for the first time introduce her brood to the pride. Walking slowly, she utters grunts—uh-uh-uh—meaning "come," and the cubs toddle behind her. Excitedly, they want to explore their new horizons, clambering up logs, investigating warthog burrows. Yet no matter how adventuresome they seem, some obscure racial wisdom urges them to stay close to their mother.

I once watched a lioness lead her three small cubs into a ravine. While she briefly drank at a pool, one cub explored on its own. It forgot its family in this wondrous new world, until suddenly it realized that it was alone. Frantically it ran back and forth calling, but the wind carried its pleas away, and its mother, unable to count to three, departed with the other cubs across the plains. She never returned to seek her off-spring.

The first momentous day away from the lair not only opens new horizons to cubs but also transforms them into truly social cats. I witnessed such an event one morning. Lioness B led her two cubs toward an acacia where members of her pride often rested. Six large cubs were waiting there, the adults not yet having returned from their night's hunt. Seeing the newcomers, the large cubs bounded up to greet them. Afraid, one small cub fled while the other hid behind its mother. The large cubs hovered around the timid newcomer, forcing their attention on it until, after an hour, it grew bold. Cautiously, it ventured a few feet toward these potential playmates, only to lose its nerve and dash back to mother, where it gained reassurance by rubbing cheeks with her. It repeated this approach and retreat several times until finally, after five hours, it triumphantly touched noses with a stranger. There would be other traumatic experiences for the cub—the first meeting with a shaggy and gruff male, the naked emotions of pride members fighting for meat—but the long, slow task of becoming a social cat had begun.

Several males may travel together as friends, or coalitions, and their combined power enables them to subdue even an adult bull buffalo, which a single lion hesitates to attack.

Several lionesses may have cubs at about the same time, and they then combine their litters and raise them communally. At this time, the cubs enter the most carefree period of their lives. Evolution, as if to compensate for its earlier slackness, now takes extra care of the cubs. Each youngster has not just one mother but several: any lioness readily permits a cub of another litter to suckle from her. Or, if a kill has been made, any mother may lead cubs to it. Thus, should a lioness lack milk or die, her cubs have foster mothers.

The Serengeti lions exert themselves as little as possible, spending about twenty hours a day resting and sleeping. The search for food may take them as little as a mile in a day and seldom more than five to six miles. Adapted to a feast-or-famine regime, they may eat nothing for days and then so gorge themselves that their bellies are grotesquely taut. Black Mane once ate seventy-three pounds of meat during a meal.

Given such a leisurely schedule, cubs have ample time for fun. Particularly at dawn and dusk, they chase each other in play through the grass, wrestling, stalking, and otherwise displaying their lust for life. Adult males are surly brutes who seldom enter into the spirit of such moments, but the females frequently join the frolic. A lioness may pummel and gently maul a cub, or perhaps cover it with her 250-pound body until it manages to wiggle free. Such play has many functions. It teaches cubs to coordinate complex movements, such as stalking. It also reinforces social bonds within the pride. Disruptive influences exist in any society; the lions' irascibility at kills is one such influence, but play may bring pride members amiably back together again.

Lion society evolved in habitats where cover is sparse and herds of prey are alert; in such circumstances, a cooperative hunt is more successful than a stalk by a solitary cat. Spotting wildebeest or other prey, the lionesses may fan out and advance silently, stalking close enough for a rush. Animals startled by one lioness often flee carelessly into the clutches of another. Cooperation also enables lions to overpower large

Taking notes as I observe the pride through a long day.

and dangerous prey: a lone lion hesitates to attack a Cape buffalo but a pride may not. Once caught, prey must be killed efficiently, the lion protecting itself from sharp hooves and horns. Such sophisticated techniques can only be learned slowly.

Until cubs are about five months old, they are content to play and absorb the affection of the pride. When they accompany a hunt, they either bumble clumsily underfoot of the stalking lionesses or remain in the rear with the males. Often, the males do not assist in the hunt at all, and this is just as well, for they are relatively slow-moving and their conspicuous manes alert the prey.

Cubs older than five months follow the hunt silently, intently listening, watching, and absorbing pride knowledge. However, they seldom take part in the communal effort until the age of at least a year. By that time, they have probably learned many special techniques—how to encircle prey cooperatively, how to strangle a large animal by biting its throat. But they still need practice to perfect them.

Once I watched one of Flop-ear's daughters snag her first kill, a Thomson's gazelle. She was fifteen months old and she sat by the carcass without eating, a surprised look on her face. In one grand moment, she had left her cubhood behind and become a full participant in pride affairs. But her period of training was far from over.

Finally, at the age of at least two and a half years, a lion youngster is ready to face the world alone. A young female usually remains in the security of her pride, but all young males take up a life of wandering until they are old and strong enough to claim a territory of their own.

Lions cooperate in raising cubs and in stalking. It therefore puzzles me why they fail to cooperate at a kill, why they fight with such primitive passion over food. The evolution of lion society seems somehow incomplete. Though lion mothers share milk, they remain possessive about meat. Cubs learn early to guard their share and to expect violent rebuffs at kills. Even as toddlers, they realize that they must fight to survive. A cub does not hesitate to give a male forty times its size a stinging blow on the nose to assert its right to a scrap of food. A large kill provides enough for everyone; the fury of snapping jaws and flashing claws represents little more than intemperate table manners.

Competition becomes serious, though, when the prey is too small to satiate all pride members. A forty-pound gazelle is a pleasant meal for just one lioness. Hoarding it jealously, she even refuses to share with her cubs, and afterward, happily glutted, she has no inclination to hunt. The cubs go hungry, and they may even starve to death. For an observer seeing cubs with flanks hollow from starvation, it is easy to reprove lionesses for their neglect. But human values are irrelevant.

My research gave me valuable insights into the evolutionary forces shaping lion society. It helped me to reshape old myths into new truths. But did I really understand lions?

One day, I was with the pride whose daily adventures had been such an important part of my life. The animals were again sprawled in the shade. Black Mane and Brown Mane were there, and so were Flop-ear and Notch, both with small cubs. Sore-ear, a longtime member of the pride, was gone, and the Old One, too. Taking the places of these dead

Teeth bared, a female warns a cub not to be too exuberant.

ones were two sleek young lionesses, Flop-ear's daughters, who had grown from tiny, wooly cubs to powerful adults. Nothing had changed; life had only renewed itself, as it would always do, forever. Perhaps some of the old myths about lions are partly right after all—at least in the long run.

[1978]

Author's note: *Life in a pride is full of stark contrasts—for example, between the joyful exuberance of cubs and the intense stalking of prey, as illustrated by two excerpts from my book* Golden Shadows, Flying Hooves.

Cubs most often played at dusk and dawn, and I eagerly looked forward to their antics. Their capacity to have fun was so infectious that it always gave me unalloyed pleasure. One day three lionesses of the Seronera pride rested while their seven cubs played around them in the grass. I kept notes on the bewildering variety of play of one of these cubs—a male, six months old. I had not named this cub, or any of the others, for the death rate of youngsters was so high that my notebooks would have consisted of obituary columns of deceased friends; I preferred to keep mere impersonal notations of demise. At any rate, the cub was now a vigorous one with a cocky expression and a slight unkempt ruff, the first intimation of his mane. These were his actions during ten minutes of play:

He pawed a twig, then chewed on it. When another cub passed by, he lunged and bit it in the lower back. The assaulted cub whirled around, slapped our hero in the face, and walked off. He sat as if planning some new devilment. Suddenly he crouched and slowly, very slowly, stalked toward an unsuspecting cub. Finally he rushed. The two tumbled over and grappled before separating amicably, our cub now biting a tuft of grass instead. Tiring of this, he flopped first on his side, then rolled on his back and waved his paws in the air.

Several cubs played near him, and these he watched intently. When one cub ambled closer, our cub hugged the ground behind a tuft of grass and waited. Bounding out of hiding with exaggerated jumps, his mouth open and lips drawn back in a smile, he swatted at one cub and after that turned on another and nipped it in the flank, a form of greeting that led to his being clouted on the head. Two cubs wrestled gently nearby and he entered the fray enthusiastically, only to be slapped in the face, rebuffed again. A cub trotted by, intent on some errand. He lunged and tried to grab it with his forepaws but missed. Both cubs then reared up on their hind legs and, leaning into each other, cuffed clumsily until the other one fell on his back, our cub on top trying to bite its throat with mock severity. Then they sat side by side, looking for new worlds to conquer, unaware that they were being stalked until our cub was hit on the head from behind. Failing to see the humor of the situation, he turned with a snarl and swiped the air in futile fury as the silent intruder vanished in the grass. He then reclined, his playful mood seemingly dampened, but suddenly he grasped a twig with both paws and bit it, shaking his head from side to side. The twig at least would not hit back.

The most common form of play among cubs consists of chasing wildly through the grass, of wrestling, pawing, and stalking. Small cubs, those less than six months old, are particularly fond of wrestling, but as cubs grow older they seem to prefer games with less body contact, such as stalking. Sometimes a cub picks up a branch and runs with it, and others then acquire an irresistible urge to possess it too, with the result that several may pursue, the chase ending with a tug-of-war during which each cub hangs on grimly as the branch is pulled this way and that.

From a cub's point of view, males must be surly brutes, for most attempts to draw them into play are rebuffed with a slap or growl. Yet cubs are strangely drawn to these strong and withdrawn members of the pride. They like to sit by males and imitate them by, for example, yawning or sharpening claws when their elders do. The lionesses are more tolerant of playing cubs than are males, although their patience must be severely tested at times. A cub may leap onto a sleeping lioness with a thump that audibly knocks the air out of her; it may drape itself over her face, almost smothering her; it may pull her leg, bite her tail, and in general make a nuisance of itself without eliciting more than a mild reprimand. In fact, a lioness may reciprocate by slapping a cub hard but with restraint, first feinting with one paw and, when the cub's attention is diverted, clouting it with the other; and she may pummel, maul, and chase it until it finally reclines on its back, exhausted, begging for peace.

At night, when the moon stares in silence at the Earth, a whole group of lions may gambol on the plains, sometimes dark shadows, sometimes shimmering silver spirits, the magic of such scenes never growing less with repetition.

Emotions cannot be re-created, but there are some hunts I remember with special clarity and feeling. One day Flop-ear plodded along the banks of the Seronera River in the midday heat. It was the dry season, and her paws raised puffs of dust. With little cover and her golden hide quite conspicuous against the gray earth, the portents for a meal were not good. The plains were empty of prey except for a few distant topi and an occasional zebra family. She met three of her friends resting beneath a tree, all contentedly full on a zebra foal they had caught just upriver. At first Flop-ear was tempted to tarry, but then she trudged on.

When she saw four zebras—three adults and a foal—approach the river in single file, heading toward a crossing, she began to slink along the dry streambed, moving closer. Once, almost imperceptibly, she raised her head to look over a tuft of grass, then continued toward a clump of reeds near the crossing. Holding her body low to the ground, she became a part of the shadows of the fever trees and she fused with the grassy stubble, flowing toward her goal. Undetected, she entered the reeds and waited. Still oblivious to danger, the zebras approached the riverbank and after a moment's hesitation walked down the gentle

A pride drinks from a temporary water puddle on a road. Lions may drink daily if water is available but can go many days without it, obtaining moisture from the carcasses of prey.

incline. The tension of watching their leisurely advance was almost unbearable for me, and I felt my muscles grow rigid as if for a rush. Suddenly the zebra last in line halted. I feared that Flop-ear had been detected and that the zebras would now wheel about and race away. But the first three animals continued on through the streambed and up the other side. One adult passed by her at a distance of thirty feet, and then the other. Last in line was the foal. A tawny flash, a violent leap, and the lioness hurtled through the air. She hit the side of the foal with a loud slap and both crashed to the ground, the air rent with its screaming. This, incidentally, was the only time I saw a lioness actually leap at her prey.

Before going to Africa I had read a number of books and articles about lions. Some authors described the wonderful way in which members of a pride cooperate while hunting their prey, yet others considered such behavior accidental or an outright myth. I too was somewhat skeptical about the existence of cooperative hunting, but to my delight some of the accounts were at least partially true. It has been said that the lionesses may hide while the male roars from the other side, thus driving the prey into the ambush. I have never seen this happen. Animals are not really afraid of a roar, unless it is exceedingly close, for, after all, once a lion reveals itself the prey is generally safe. Furthermore, a male rarely participates in a collaborative effort; he is likely to wreck a carefully laid ambush by indifferently startling the prey. Lionesses, however, may use quite sophisticated techniques when hunting together, each watching the others and patterning her actions to suit the situation.

One morning lionesses Nos. 69 and 102 of the Cub Valley group were resting on a promontory when they saw two wildebeest bulls wending their way along a reedbed in their direction. Immediately descending from her vantage point and moving swiftly in a semi-crouch, No. 69 crossed the reeds, halting to look back at the friend following in her tracks. She then crept over a strip of hard-packed clay into a patch of tall grass, where she flattened to the ground. No. 102 hid herself at the edge of the reeds, facing the other lioness. If the wildebeest held to their course they would be neatly trapped between the two cats. The lead animal stopped abruptly sixty feet from the ambush and glanced back at his companion as if checking to see if he sensed danger too. At that, lioness No. 69 rushed, streaking forward fast and low.

Wheeling, dodging, and accelerating in one frantic series of movements, the wildebeest fled. One of them, for some reason, ran into the reeds, where in the thick vegetation it lost speed. Even so, its escape seemed assured until suddenly its forelegs dropped into a hole. Before he could fully regain his feet, one lioness grasped him by the neck and bit at his throat while the other straddled his back. Slowly all sank out of sight among the reeds and I could hear only the disembodied growls of lions on a kill.

[1973]

A Movable Feast

Wildebeest

My project in the Serengeti attempted to answer one main question: what effect does predation have on prey populations? I focused on the lion as the principal predator, while Hans Kruuk concentrated on the spotted hyena; others at the Serengeti Research Institute studied various ungulate species, particularly the great migration of wildebeest.

Migratory species such as wildebeest, Mongolian gazelles, and at one time bison dominate their ungulate communities by their sheer numbers. Why are they so abundant? As noted by John Fryxell and A. R. E. Sinclair, wildebeest and other migrants have greater access to abundant and nutritious forage than residents because they inhabit larger areas, use resources more efficiently by shifting to new ranges, and are less vulnerable to predation. Tied to territories and small cubs, most lions cannot follow the moving herds, nor can most hyenas. Consequently predators kill relatively few wildebeest, with lions and hyenas each taking only 2 to 3 percent of the population annually. The survival of wildebeest is most strongly influenced by available food during the dry season, when grass is so low in nutrients that it may not meet energy requirements. By contrast, resident prey such as impala, warthogs, and hartebeests are regulated more than the wildebeest by predation. Diseases also kill wildebeest, as does pure negligence: one herd needlessly crossed shallow, muddy Lake Lagaja, and 685 calves floundered and died.

❧

Wildebeest pervade the Serengeti by their sheer numbers. Though predators may have the most visual impact on visitors, it is the huge, amorphous mass of the wildebeest population that permeates the thoughts of residents. Either the animals are present, inundating an area with black bodies, the air trembling with their grunts, or they are conspicuously absent, not a single individual as a reminder that the species exists. Bernhard Grzimek, Lee Talbot, and Murray Watson have outlined the general pattern of wildebeest movements. From the plains the animals sweep westward into the Corridor [the narrow western portion of the park], where the herds break up and move in small groups north toward the Kenya border. There they tarry until once again rains signal them to return to the plains.

Why do they surge back to the plains at the first opportunity, leaving behind ample grass? Perhaps the short species of grass are particularly nutritious. It is also possible that tradition plays an important role in their movements. Wildebeest prefer open habitats, and the eastern plains may have been their ancient ground when the rest of the Serengeti was more densely wooded and provided only a temporary retreat in seasons of exceptional dryness. Whatever the reason, their movement may be essential to the well-being of the grasslands. Hubert Braun, a Dutch botanist who with good-natured resignation always identified the wilted and battered remnants of plants I brought to him for identification, studied forage production in the park. He found that if he repeatedly clipped his experimental grass plots on the eastern plains at varying intervals, the total yields were the same for each plot. However, in the long-grass areas, which cover the western plains and woodlands, the yield decreased sharply with the frequency of cutting, indicating that if all the wildebeest and zebras were to remain in these areas throughout the year, the range might well deteriorate under the constant heavy grazing.

The wildebeest is a strangely fashioned antelope, seemingly assembled from the leavings in some evolutionary factory. Its head is heavy

The immense herds of Serengeti wildebeest are one of the greatest spectacles in nature. Over a million animals may crowd the plains in season; during migration the herds surge ahead, across and through obstacles such as rivers. Some in the massed throng may drown, providing easy meals for crocodiles.

and blunt, and it has a shaggy white beard and knobby, curving horns that give it a petulant mien. Its stringy black mane is so sparse that it seems to compensate for this thinness by having several vertical black slashes on its neck, an arrangement comparable to someone simulating a toupee by drawing black lines on his pate. The bulky shoulders give way to spindly hindquarters and a plumed tail that flails about as if with a will of its own. Wildebeest alone seem rather woeful, but en masse they convey a strange beauty and power. Occasionally I walked among them. Retreating a few hundred feet to let me pass, the animals near me stood silently, their horns shining in the sun. Those farther back continued their incessant grunting, sounding like a chorus of monstrous frogs. Now and then several animals dashed off in apparent panic only to halt and stare back at me. The air was heavy with odor—of earth and manure and trampled grass.

Tens of thousands of young are born on the plains at the same time, within a period of about two weeks, offering a superabundance of vulnerable prey to lions, hyenas, and wild dogs.

Wildebeest herds on the march are at their most impressive. Trudging along in single file or several abreast, they move in a hunched gait, only to break suddenly into a lope as they pour over hills and funnel down valleys, herd after herd, a living black flood tracing the age-old trails of their predecessors. This immutable urge to stay with the herd, to move in the direction of the others, causes them to press forward regardless of obstacles in their path. One day several lionesses settled by a brushy ravine that had been crossed by several herds during their erratic trek. In the course of a few hours the lionesses captured six wildebeest, yet after hesitating briefly, each succeeding herd rushed recklessly ahead, deterred neither by the bodies of their compatriots nor by the smell of blood and lions.

If a river bars their way, they plunge in, disregarding all dangers, and many may drown. One day I watched about a thousand wildebeest gallop in a long line toward the Seronera River, a mindless mass in motion seemingly without reason or purpose. Those in the lead hurled themselves down the embankment, hit the water, and swam to the opposite side where its steepness halted them. The horde swept in behind, and soon the water was crowded with thrashing animals, rearing up, climbing over each other, desperate in their attempts to scramble up the slippery sides. Some were pushed under so far that only their noses and bared white incisors were visible as they strained to stay above water. High-pitched bleats reached a frantic crescendo when those in front turned and met the rest still pressing ahead. Finally some gained the far bank, and the others surged back past me with frantic, rolling eyes, still racing with implacable urgency except that now they headed in the direction from which they had just come. Seven dark bodies floating silently in the river attested to their violent passing. . . .

The August rains in 1966 were not widespread enough to permit the migratory herds to move out to the plains. The skies cleared and the dry season continued unabated through October. Some rain usually falls in November and December, and this enables the animals to venture from the woodlands. According to expectation, storms burst over much of the park in early November, but rushing to the woodlands' edge, the herds met only desiccated grass. They milled and waited, but not until mid-December were they able to leave the trees behind. A week later they were forced to retreat, the green grass gone, the sun blazing out of a clear sky once more. January came and went, and still dust hovered over the parched earth. Animals were lethargic, plants dormant, people irritable, as everything waited for the rain to continue the usual rhythm of life.

Most wildebeest calves are born in late January and February. In 1967, for the first time in years, the wildebeest had to calve in the woodlands. Their calving season is one of the most inspiring and at the same time most tragic spectacles in the Serengeti. I watched one cow give birth, remaining far from her but with my eye steady on the scope until it ceased to exist and I became part of the scene. She stood quietly, breathing heavily. Soon two feet appeared, the hooves strikingly pale, and then the head and body encased in a luminous gray sheath. It dropped limply onto the grass, breaking the cord, and the cow lowered her broad muzzle to nibble at the fetal membranes and then lick the wet hide. Within seconds the calf raised its head and, seeing its mother looming above, tried to rise. Shakily it raised its rump, toppled, tried again with the same result. But its racial wisdom urged it to struggle on, to gain its feet at all costs, until finally it stood unsteadily, legs spread and body weaving, a personal victory that I silently cheered. It fell again and again, yet each time regained its feet with greater ease. Within ten minutes after birth it stumbled along, its frail body pressed to the side of its mother. This calf aroused little interest in the other wildebeest, but those born early in the season often receive the fascinated attention of yearlings and adults. Crowding around, they gently butt the new arrival, sniff it, or perhaps buck and abruptly leap backward. The first commandment of a calf is to get on its feet, the second to remain close to its mother. With herds large and constantly on the move, a calf that becomes separated from its mother by even fifty feet may never see her again. No cow will accept a stranger, and as an outcast among the multitude, a lost calf slowly dies of starvation unless rescued from this fate by a predator.

Cows with small calves tend to aggregate into highly skittish herds. Tourists drive unheedingly through such herds and planes buzz them, spreading confusion and panic, during which some calves invariably become lost. For these and other reasons, orphans are a common sight. A lost youngster at first dashes back and forth frantically bleating, but its voice is lost in the rumble of pounding hooves; it repeatedly runs up to strange wildebeest only to be rebuffed with a butt. Exhausted, the calf finally falters in its determination to join someone, and while the others recede into the distance, trailing a vane of dust, it halts, a small light-brown spot alone on the immensity of the plain. However, its urge to follow something, anything, is strong. I have seen calves attach themselves to zebras and eland, plodding behind the herd, quite ignored. The

Wild dogs have isolated and attacked this yearling wildebeest.

first time I took Kay to see the wildebeest herds massed near Naabi Hill, an orphan galloped up to our car as if this steel monster were its mother. Kay all but burst into tears at the sight of the forlorn animal, and when by the end of our day she had met several more such youngsters, she refused to ever visit the calving herds again.

Once a lost calf trailed two male lions for one and a half miles, trotting eagerly to within fifty feet of them. One or the other of the males made futile attempts to grab it, but heeding its inborn warning to avoid anything that approaches rapidly, it lightly sidestepped the lunges. When the lions resumed their walk, it trailed them once more. The lions then reclined and the calf, losing interest in them, drifted onto a rise. And there, on the opposite side of a gentle valley, stood another orphan. Excitedly the calf looked toward this potential friend and with a burst of exuberance ran toward it, ran on in its escape from loneliness, oblivious to everything, even the lionesses that rose as if out of the ground and after a brief chase pulled it down. As the lioness held its throat until the new life faded from its eyes, hopefully the last thing it remembered was the other calf also hurrying to this ill-fated rendezvous.

At the height of the birth season the predators and scavengers can for once eat to satiation. Hyenas waddle along with their bellies almost touching the ground, lions stand panting, unable to recline comfortably on the monstrous bulge of their abdomen, and vultures flap awkwardly near carcasses, too full of offal to ride the currents into the air. Man sees himself reflected in nature, and conscious of my ties to a hunting life, I could not but find satisfaction in the repletion of these animals.

[1973]

An Elegant Cat

Cheetah

The social system of cheetahs was not yet clear when my Serengeti years concluded. However, long-term work by Tim Caro and others shows clearly that males are territorial, defending areas as small as fifteen square miles, but also that two or three males may cooperate in maintaining that territory. By contrast, females are nomadic and solitary, roaming over areas of as much as five hundred square miles. No wonder that months sometimes passed during which I did not meet certain cheetahs.

At present the cheetah is Africa's most endangered large cat. Perhaps twelve thousand to fifteen thousand survive as small, scattered populations in twenty-nine countries. (The Asiatic cheetah is extinct except for about sixty in Iran.) Ranchers kill the cat, habitat is converted to farmland, and lions, spotted hyenas, and leopards prey on cheetahs. In the Serengeti, only about 5 percent of cubs reach maturity because of an increase in hyenas. As if fate had not burdened the cheetah enough, Stephen O'Brien discovered that individual cats are genetically almost identical to each other. Such lack of genetic diversity may have serious consequences for a species. Inbreeding may lead to birth defects, reduction in fertility, a weak immune defense system against disease, and—so important in this age of global warming—a lack of adaptability to environmental change. None of these symptoms has as yet appeared in the cheetah, but I watch its race for survival with anxiety, as well as with guilt that my species has so persecuted this graceful icon of our natural world.

꒜

With its small round head, trim waist, and long, slender legs, the cheetah is the most atypical of the cats, an animal built for speed, a greyhound with the coat of a leopard. A delicate and aristocratic animal, it seems to belong with royalty; indeed, trained cheetahs were used as early as 365 B.C. by King Hashing of Persia to hunt gazelle. In the sixteenth century the Mogul emperor Akbar the Great of India is said to have kept one thousand cheetahs. A hooded cat would be transported in a bullock cart to within three hundred feet of a herd of blackbuck antelope. With the hood removed, the cheetah slipped off the cart, crept closer, and finally sprinted after the prey. If it missed, the keeper came up, chanting, "Oh, great King, do not be angry, you will kill the next one," as he slipped the hood over the cat's eyes. But if it captured an adult male, as it was taught to do, success was rewarded by a cup of blood from the slain animal.

Today this sport is extinct in India and so is the cheetah—the last one was shot there in 1952. A few survive in Iran and some possibly in the Baluchistan province of Pakistan. Strays show up occasionally in North Africa. Fortunately cheetahs are still widespread in the open woodlands and plains south of the Sahara, where suitable prey survive. But they are nowhere abundant, not even in the national parks. The five thousand square miles of the Serengeti in Tanzania contain perhaps 150 cheetahs, one per thirty-three square miles; the large Kruger National Park in South Africa has about one per twenty-seven square miles.

Considering the long contact that man has had with the cheetah, remarkably little was known of its habits until recently. Aloof and self-contained, it remained an enigma, even refusing to breed in captivity. Among Emperor Akbar's thousand cheetahs, only one had young, a litter of three. No other captive births were reported until 1956, and since then only seven litters have been born in zoos. [Captive breeding efforts have improved greatly in recent years.] When I joined the Serengeti Research Institute in 1966 to study predators, particularly the lion, in the

Serengeti National Park, I became intrigued by the cheetah, not only by its mystery but also by its delicate beauty and lithe grace.

Most Serengeti cheetahs are migratory, following the movements of their principal prey, the Thomson's gazelle. During the rains early in the year, when the gazelles are on the plains, the cheetahs are there too, but when the grass dries up in July, both move twenty-five or more miles to the edge of the acacia woodlands that cover much of the park. There some cheetahs remain for several months. Occasionally one stays within a three- to four-square-mile area for a month, but usually each uses some twenty to twenty-five square miles of terrain in the course of a season. The same cheetah tends to return yearly to the same locality, and one of my pleasures was to recognize an individual after a long absence.

Cheetahs do not establish territories in the sense of defending a locality against other cheetahs. Several animals commonly range over the same area, but they avoid contact. When two see each other, they

A cheetah female drags her gazelle kill toward her waiting cubs. A cheetah must kill about a gazelle per day if she has large cubs to feed. The main prey of cheetahs in the Serengeti is the Thomson's gazelle.

veer apart without associating. Cheetahs also squirt a mixture of scent and urine against tree trunks and often deposit their feces on prominent locations such as termite mounds. A cheetah that smells a fresh marker knows that the area has been visited recently and can then plan its movements to avoid a meeting. Cheetahs do not advertise their presence by roaring in the manner of lions. Their only calls are a birdlike chirp and a sedate staccato chirr used mainly to keep mother and cubs in contact with each other.

It has often been said that adult cheetahs are sociable and travel mainly in groups. I found this infrequently in the Serengeti. Excluding mothers with cubs, 52 percent of my sightings were of solitary individuals, 31 percent of the cheetahs were in pairs, and the rest were in groups of three to four. Two or three adult males sometimes became companions for months, but I never saw two adult females in a group. Adult males and females associated mainly during courtship. Although I frequently saw groups of two to four males and females, these were with few exceptions litters of grown cubs that had not yet split up. The extent to which female cheetahs are asocial was shown well by a mother and her two grown daughters. Although all three wandered over the same area and sometimes saw each other, to my knowledge they never met.

This particular family provided me with some of my most interesting observations on cheetah life history. The mother gave birth to at least three cubs in July 1967, in a jumble of granite boulders and brush. By September she had only two cubs left. Most cheetahs lose about half of their cubs as a result of illness, predation, or abandonment, but a few manage to raise whole litters of four to five. Her cubs, like those of all cheetahs, were black with a long blue-gray mantle of hair on their heads and backs, a striking natal coat that is lost at about three months. The cubs began to follow her around when they were about six weeks old; at three months they ceased to suckle. They were a close-knit family and shared kills without fighting. After a meal they licked each other's faces, purring loudly. Yet somehow their social existence seemed constrained; it lacked that intense quality of contact found among lions and even leopards. Perhaps it was because cheetahs do not rub their cheeks and bodies sinuously together in greeting, as lions and other cats do. Perhaps their tenuous social contacts as adults make an intimate bond between mother and offspring irrelevant. In fact, one observation suggests that mothers cannot recognize their young when they are small. Once two mothers, each with two cubs about three months old, met inadvertently at a kill, then parted after briefly threatening each other. But one cub followed the wrong mother. She noticed the addition but could not distinguish the newcomer from her own. She cuffed any cub that approached her until all three cringed, and she refused to associate with them for at least eight hours. I was afraid that she would abandon all of them. Somehow the extra cub was reunited with its mother that night.

How to hunt was perhaps the most important lesson these cubs had to learn while still with their mother. At first they played around her while she stalked, sometimes alerting the prey by running ahead. But later, at about three months of age, a change occurred. They followed discreetly or watched while she hunted. A female may even provide her cubs with the opportunity to learn the techniques of killing. My wife, Kay, watched a cheetah carry a live gazelle fawn to her five-month-old cubs and release it. They tried to capture it, and once they knocked it down but were unable to kill it. Finally the mother did so. At the age of about one year, cubs themselves will initiate some hunts. For example, in August 1968, when she was thirteen months old, a cub of the litter I had observed for over a year bowled over a gazelle fawn several times with a swat of her paw. But she was so inept at grabbing it that finally the mother ran up and killed it. In three subsequent hunts the mother took the initiative. On October 1, when they were almost fifteen months old, the cubs bungled yet another hunt, only to be helped again by their mother.

Some two weeks later, on October 17, the family was still together, but on the following day the cubs separated permanently from their mother. It was a sudden and dramatic break, especially considering the cubs' inability to hunt well. There was no gradual severing of the social

Cheetahs often have three cubs, but fewer than 10 percent of all cubs survive to become adults because so many are killed by lions and other predators.

bonds, no tentative, solitary excursions, just an abrupt transition from dependence to complete independence. These cubs never again associated with their mother. Other litters behaved similarly. In contrast, the leopard, another solitary cat, behaves in a more typical manner. One female cub whose history I traced from birth began to occasionally roam on her own at the age of thirteen months, but continued to meet and share kills with her mother until she was twenty-two months old. Three months later her mother conceived again.

The two cheetah sisters lost weight after separating from their mother, but they survived, and with the onset of the rains they moved to the plains. By February 1969, they too had split up, for I met one as I was walking across the plains. She lay on her side, looking around with raised head in the curiously detached manner of cheetahs. I sat down 100 feet from her and fifteen minutes later heard a gazelle fawn bleat. Then over a rise came two jackals in pursuit of the fawn. The cheetah sprinted past me, knocked the fawn down, and grabbed it by the neck. She had obviously learned to hunt. As she ate I moved slowly toward her, finally reclining fifteen feet away. She stared at me with guileless amber eyes but did not flee. We stayed together for over half an hour, once only ten feet apart, one of my most memorable experiences with a wild animal.

One of these young females conceived in April 1969, when twenty-one months old, and her sister courted in May. A tame but free-living cheetah raised by Joy Adamson also bred at the age of twenty-two months for the first time. On July 12, I found the litter of the first young female: four cubs only a day or two old, with eyes still closed, weighing a mere twelve ounces each. They lay in a patch of grass six miles from the place where their mother had been born two years earlier. She was just moving the cubs to a thicket nine hundred feet away, carrying them one at a time by the back of a leg. After all had been moved, she returned twice more and searched the site, seemingly unable to count with precision. At the age of three weeks the cubs could walk unsteadily. On August 19, the photographer Simon Trevor saw her take the cubs to their first kill. The gazelle was not dead and the cubs were obviously frightened, jumping back each time it kicked. Another generation had to learn to become predators.

The hunt of a cheetah is surely one of the most exciting spectacles in Africa—the slow stalk, the tense period of waiting until the prey is inattentive, and finally the explosive rush at speeds of at least sixty miles per hour, making the cheetah the fastest of all land mammals. Cheetahs may hunt at any time during the day, and on moonlit nights as well, but usually they do so between 7:00 and 10:00 A.M. and 4:00 to 6:00 P.M. They seldom work hard for their meals, but lie in the shade, seemingly waiting for prey to drift into the vicinity. Or from a termite hill, they scan the horizon for prey and then slowly walk in its direction. At some time between spotting a possible quarry and chasing it, the cheetah selects one, and I was particularly interested to find out what determined that choice.

Size of prey was obviously one factor. In the parts of the Serengeti where I observed cheetahs. Thomson's gazelle was the preferred prey (91 percent), followed by Grant's gazelle, wildebeest, impala, and hare in that order. A Thomson's gazelle weighs some 35 to 40 pounds, just one large meal for a cheetah weighing 110 to 130 pounds. Adult Grant's gazelles, impala, and reedbucks were also killed, but of the wildebeest only calves were captured. Similarly, some 68 percent of the cheetah kills reported from Kruger National Park consisted of impala, and most of the other prey was relatively small too. A cheetah hunting alone seldom preys on anything weighing much more than itself, and this limits it to the small antelope and the young of the large ones. But several cheetahs together may attack a large animal, as in Nairobi National Park, where four males killed kongonis and zebras.

Prey selection can operate in two ways. In one, the predator chooses a particular animal out of a herd—a sick or newborn one—and pursues it, ignoring all others. In the other, the prey selects against itself, so to speak, by becoming vulnerable in some way. Leopards, for example, catch nearly twice as many adult male Thomson's gazelles as would be expected from the number of adult males in the population. These seem to be mostly nonterritorial males that roam through high grass and along river courses where leopards hunt, in contrast to females and territorial males, which remain in areas of short grass where they are not so vulnerable to leopards.

Cheetahs hunt mainly in the open plains. There they catch about 30 percent fewer adult male gazelles than expected, possibly because cheetahs prefer to select prey that is fleeing rather than standing around alertly as territorial males do. I collected and aged the jaws of 163 gazelle kills. The cheetahs had captured many fawns less than six months old, whereas yearlings, nine to twenty-four months old, were almost immune to predation. The cheetahs took many adults, but no age class was particularly selected. Most of the adult prey taken were presumably healthy, although the cats may have been able to detect slight disabilities that I could not. Gazelles sometimes suffer from heavy infestations of lungworm or sarcoptic mange, and such animals possibly respond less briskly to the cheetah. However, when the ages of gazelles killed by cheetahs are compared with those killed by lions, it is obvious that the two cats select very similarly. A lion captures its prey by surprise in a short fast rush, during which there is little or no time to test for weakness in an individual. In contrast, the cheetah may take its prey with a long run. Despite the two cats' different hunting techniques, the adult gazelles they killed had a similar age structure, except that lions kill fewer small young and more yearlings. Possibly cheetahs catch the sick, and lions the healthy, but I am inclined to think that most prey selected by both species were in reasonably good condition.

When observing a cheetah hunt, the selection for fawns is obvious—any fawn in a herd is immediately pursued. This is not surprising when hunting success is considered. Although cheetahs can attain tremendous speed, they are unable to keep it up for more than about nine hundred feet. If the gazelle dodges several times, the cheetah, exhausted, may have to give up the chase, and twenty-three out of twenty-six unsuccessful hunts that I observed failed for that reason. A fawn can run neither fast nor far, and in thirty-one chases after them, the cheetah was successful every time after an average run of six hundred feet. On the other hand, of fifty-six pursuits after large young and adults, only 54 percent resulted in a kill after a chase up to some nine hundred feet. Cheetahs are pragmatists: better a small meal than none at all.

Cheetahs prefer to hunt a solitary individual or one in a small herd, because they have difficulty selecting a gazelle and keeping it in sight in a large, milling herd. Individuals are chosen that enter tall grass, graze behind some bushes, or otherwise enable the cheetah to stalk undetected. With endless patience the cat may wait for a gazelle to lower its head and graze while briefly facing away from the danger, thus giving the cheetah an undetected second during the rush—often the difference between success and failure. The selection process is not always an easy one. Cheetahs sometimes bound toward a herd, then give up for no obvious reason, probably because they are unable to find a suitable quarry. Or they first pursue a herd at moderate speed before suddenly making a selection. Here are two typical hunts:

A female cheetah climbs 10 feet up a tree and spots ten gazelles about 700 feet away. She approaches the herd slowly, with head held low, until she is some 300 feet from the animals. She sits and watches for five minutes. One gazelle grazes somewhat apart from the herd. The cheetah rushes and is within 100 feet before the gazelle flees. After a chase of about 480 feet, which includes a sharp 180-degree turn, the gazelle flips forward, tripped by the cheetah, which lunges in and grabs the throat. After five minutes, the gazelle dies from strangulation.

A female cheetah spots a dozen gazelles on a burned stubble 800 feet away. She slowly walks 300 feet toward them; then, at a moderate speed, she bounds about 500 feet before selecting the smallest individual in the fleeing herd. She sprints after it, follows three zigzags closely, and after 400 feet catches it in a cloud of dust. She emerges holding it by the throat.

After knocking a gazelle down by hitting its flank or rump with a paw, the cheetah typically grabs it by the throat and throttles it, a task that requires four and a half minutes on the average. The carcass is often dragged to a shady spot. Cheetahs usually eat the meat off one thigh first; after that they cut the meat from the abdomen and rib cage, sometimes stopping to lap up any blood that collects in the body cavity. Finally they strip the rest of the meat from the inside. All that generally remains is the articulated skeleton with much of the skin and the whole digestive tract. The cats eat rapidly, glancing nervously around at intervals. This is not surprising, for lions, hyenas, and other predators often arrive at the kill, having been alerted by descending vultures that a meal is in the offing. Cheetahs are timid creatures, low in the predator hierarchy, and 12 percent of their kills end in someone else's stomach. Twice I saw a cheetah driven from its kill by a solid phalanx of vultures. The cheetahs did little to retaliate when their kill was scavenged except to hiss and moan in a peculiar manner, although one bold hyena was slapped in the face.

A cheetah chases a white-backed vulture from the vicinity of its kill after the impatient bird came too close.

To find out how often a cheetah kills, several persons with the Serengeti Research Institute and I watched a female with two small cubs for twenty-six days. There is a primitive pleasure in spending a day with a predator. Nothing happens for hours. The plains shimmer with heat waves. Yet there is a tension in the air, a feeling of impending violence. During these twenty-six days the cheetah killed twenty-four Thomson's gazelles, ranging from small fawns to adults, and one hare. At this rate she would kill 337 gazelles per year. She caught nothing on three days, although she tried, but on two days she captured two gazelles each. She captured an average of 22 pounds of animal per day, but she lost two kills to lions and one to hyenas. About 40 percent of the weight of a carcass was not eaten, mainly the digestive tract and bones. This left about 111 pounds of meat for the mother and two cubs, almost twice as much as she actually needed, judging by the amount fed to cheetahs in zoos. Other mothers killed equally often, but solitary cheetahs captured prey probably only once every two to three days. Taking into account the size of the cheetah population, the percentage of gazelle in their diet, and other factors, it seems likely that the Serengeti cheetahs kill 15,000–20,000 gazelles a year, only a small percentage of the several hundred thousand gazelles in the park.

Given such a large amount of prey and their success in catching it, there were surprisingly few cheetahs in the park. The Nairobi National Park, only forty-four square miles in size, usually had some ten to fifteen resident cheetahs, showing that the species can tolerate quite high densities. Adult females outnumbered males by a ratio of two to one, and one-third of the females were accompanied by cubs, often large ones. Females that lose their litter may come into estrus again within a week, and the gestation period is only ninety to ninety-five days. The Serengeti cheetahs have a high reproductive potential, a satisfactory number of cubs are raised, and food seems to be no problem. Yet something keeps the population depressed at a low level. A leopard killed and stored a cheetah in a tree, several lions captured and strangled one, and a litter burned in a grass fire, but such deaths were insignificant to the total cheetah population.

The wild dog, an equally rare predator in the park, provided a hint. These pack-living predators raised large litters, but canine distemper killed over half the members of one pack and undoubtedly affected other packs as well. During my stay in the Serengeti the wild dog population did not increase. It had failed to increase since at least 1956, the period for which there is information. The dog population seems to be controlled by disease, not by the food supply. Possibly cheetahs are also affected by disease, although I have no evidence to show this. The basic question of just what factors operate on the dog and cheetah populations to keep them stable at such a low level remains unanswered. Disease can cause a decrease, but something else must finally determine that level at which the population stabilizes.

The cheetah is uncommon to rare everywhere, and the species balances itself delicately between security and extinction in an area. Any additional mortality, such as shooting by man, may well have a serious effect on a population. Yet in 1966, seventy-five cheetah coats were sold in New York alone to satisfy the vanity of a few women. A total of 3,168 cheetah skins were imported into the United States in 1968–69, as many as would normally be found in 98,525 square miles of Africa, given the densities in Kruger and Serengeti National Parks. Unless the cheetah is more strictly protected, this gentle and elegant cat will surely follow its Asian cousin toward extinction over much of Africa.

[1970]

SOUTH ASIA,
CHINA, AND MONGOLIA

It ill becomes us to invoke in our daily prayers the blessings of God, the Compassionate, if we in turn do not practice elementary compassion towards our fellow creatures.

—Mahatma Gandhi

Heaven and earth and I coexist.
The world and I are one.

—Zhuang Zi, Chinese philosopher, 369–286 B.C.

Light in the Forest

Tiger

The massive power, dignity, and flaming beauty of the tiger had burned itself into my being when I concluded my study of the Indian tiger in 1965, but at the time few persons in that country cared about observing the cat, except along the barrel of a rifle. Prime Minister Indira Gandhi changed attitudes when she vigorously promoted protection of wildlife and forests, showing well how a perceptive and caring leader can benefit a nation's future. Tiger shooting was banned in 1970, and "Project Tiger" was initiated in 1973 with a core group of protected areas that now number twenty-seven. Field biologists, among them Ullas Karanth of the Wildlife Conservation Society and Raghumandan Chundawat, established a scientific basis for studying and censusing tigers; while Valmik Thapar, Fateh Singh Rathore, and Belinda Wright, to name just three of the tiger's champions, have fought with persistence to halt poaching and educate the public about the cat's spiritual and cultural values.

Tigers once roamed unhampered from Turkey to the Russian Far East. Today at most 5,000 to 7,500 may remain, half of them in India. Hunting tigers is banned in all countries, in Bangladesh since 1968 and India since 1970. Yet many forest tracts are now empty of tigers and their prey, and their numbers continue to dwindle because of poaching. Even tigers in reserves are not safe: in 2004 many tigers that were well known to visitors in India's famous Panna and Ranthambhore reserves suddenly vanished, and they were entirely wiped out in the Sariska reserve. The cats are shot, trapped, or poisoned—sometimes because they kill livestock but now more often because their bones and other body parts *are used in traditional medicines or as luxury furs in China, Korea, and else-where. As recently as 2003, Chinese customs officials confiscated a shipment from India with 32 tiger skins, 581 leopard skins, and 778 otter skins destined for Tibet, where local people use them to trim their garments. Tigers are adapt-able and resilient, and they are still found in fourteen countries, but they cannot long withstand such persecution. Yet the situation is not wholly bleak, and tigers can continue to burn bright in the forests if countries devote willpower and long-term commitment to their survival.*

Stan Wayman and I crouched in the darkness and listened to the sounds of tigers on a kill—the growls, snarls, and grating of tooth on bone—making the walls of our grass blind seem thin indeed. Every few seconds our glade was flooded with a brilliant flash from the strobe lights attached to the surrounding trees and synchronized with Stan's camera. Each time, for a fleeting moment, we saw the tigers "burning bright in the forests of the night," to quote the apt words of William Blake.

There were four tigers—three females and a male of one litter—not quite fully grown but, at almost one and a half years of age, impres-sively large. They crowded around the domestic buffalo we had given them, bolting down the meat as if unaware of our presence a hundred feet away.

Flashes of lightning from an approaching storm began to mingle with those of our strobe lights. Even one drop of rain would cause a hot bulb to explode, ruining all further chances for night photography here in the remote Kanha National Park of Central India.

"We've got to get those lights down," whispered Stan urgently. We stepped from the blind and walked slowly toward the tigers. "Go away, tigers, go away," I said in a tense voice as I held the cats in the beam of my small flashlight, and Stan clapped his hands several times. The tigers reluctantly retreated. I stood by their kill, the air saturated with the

Tigers like to remain cryptic, and they may be difficult to spot in dense vegetation.

heavy odor of blood, pointing the flashlight alternately at Stan collecting the bulbs and at the tigers sitting scattered in the grass some forty feet away, their shining eyes fixed on us. Hurriedly we returned to our blind, and the tigers resumed their meal.

For over two weeks we lived in that blind. Stan had joined me to photograph the tigers on an assignment for *Life* while I completed a research project on the cats. We became friends during those days, a bond forged by the sympathetic sharing of such experiences as rescuing the strobe lights and listening to the tigers as they stealthily circled our blind at night, the dry grass barely crackling beneath their paws. These weeks also marked the end of my wildlife studies in Kanha Park, where my family and I had lived for over a year. The tigers were all old friends whom I had met many times before; they were used to people near their kill.

I remember well the first time I saw this litter of tigers, when, twelve months earlier, the youngsters were the size of small setter dogs.

The mother had killed a bull gaur—a species of wild cattle—in a ravine, and she was camped with her cubs by the carcass. During the cool mornings the cubs sometimes played, stalking each other clumsily, wrestling, and chasing. Then, during the heat of the day, they rested contentedly.

The tigress often cooled herself by reclining with her hindquarters submerged in a pool. As the forest grew dark, the family resumed its meal. I watched them from the branches of a nearby tree, lithe shadows under a crescent moon.

The tiger family I observed feasted on their gaur for five consecutive nights. On one of these, at 4:30 A.M., the tigress roared twice: *Aa-uu, aa-uu*. An answer came from far away. Who was it, I wondered? This tigress confined her wanderings to about twenty-five square miles of woodlands and meadows in the center of the park, a home range that she shared, however, with three other tigresses and a male. The roars signified "I am here," and the two tigers now knew of each other's whereabouts; they had the choice of meeting or avoiding each other.

This time they chose the former course, for at 8:00 A.M. the male tiger, a huge fellow with a short ruff of hair on his neck, suddenly appeared. He ambled casually along the edge of the ravine, secure in the power of his rule over this part of the park. The two tigers met silently behind a bush, both partially hidden from view, and remained there for three minutes, then parted amicably.

Later in the year, when the cubs were nine months old, the tigress killed a buffalo just before 8:00 P.M. and after a brief snack left to fetch her cubs. An hour and a half later, swamp deer and axis deer barked in alarm, and I knew that the tigers were approaching. Soon the cubs appeared and rushed exuberantly to the kill. Then the tigress arrived, closely followed by the male tiger.

Somewhere on a forest trail they had met. The male's lean abdomen showed that he had not killed anything for several days, yet he did not eat. Patiently he waited by the carcass. Satiated, the tigress lay down beside him, and then a cub did too, first rubbing its face against his, the typical greeting between cats. Finally, after two and a half hours of waiting, the male took his first bite.

From these and other observations emerged a new and unexpected picture of the tiger's social life. Adult tigers have traditionally been regarded as solitary, irascibly avoiding all contact except when mating. While it is true that tigers usually roam alone, they do meet now and then, sometimes casually on a trail, at other times to share a kill. In fact, the resident tigers in my study area were part of a small community in which all members knew each other.

One night I saw the male, the tigress with four cubs, and another tigress with one cub, a total of seven, together on a kill. But by morning they had separated again—solitary but certainly not unsociable. In addition, wanderers, tigers without a settled home, drifted into the area, stayed briefly, and moved on, their fate a mystery to me.

Though generally alone, tigers are well aware of others in the vicinity, for each animal leaves behind signs of its presence. Sometimes a tiger stops and rakes its hindpaws alternately on the ground, making a conspicuous scrape and often adding a bit of feces. Occasionally, too, a tiger squirts urine mixed with scent backward against bushes and trees along its route of travel, an olfactory signal that for days to come will reveal to other tigers not only that someone has passed but probably also when it passed, who it was, and if a tigress, whether she was in heat.

From examinations of tiger spoor, and the hair in the droppings, I learned what the tigers had eaten, and thus the importance of various prey species. The composition of the droppings was axis deer (52 percent), sambar deer, swamp deer, gaur, domestic cow, and buffalo (each about 8 percent), langur monkey (6 percent), and the rest such miscellaneous items as porcupine, frog, and grass. An examination of kills showed that many killed animals were either young or old; tigers, like many other predators, catch whatever is easiest, mainly the slow and weak.

Livestock is not an important food in the center of Kanha Park, but in other areas, where wildlife has been largely exterminated, it may

*A female tiger with four large cubs (a male and three females) was in Kanha while
I was there from 1963 to 1965, and I observed these animals often. The male cub
left his family to become independent before the female cubs did so. The photo shows
this female (at left) with one of her cubs.*

provide the only available meat. Villagers naturally resent having their
animals killed, but reactions to marauding tigers vary. Many observers
describe a curious indifference, almost a tolerance, of Indians toward
resident tigers. Their half-hearted attempts to rid their area of the cats
may stem from the Eastern fatalistic attitude that pervades many aspects
of life.

It is apparent, however, that not all Indians are willing to accept
losses to tigers as easily. Now that pesticides are becoming available,
resourceful villagers are quick to see their potential; sometimes they slip
a little insecticide into a carcass, and the tiger dies a painful death. In
1969, thirty-two tigers were found dead from poison in one district alone.

Poisoning, illegal and legal hunting, the demands by the fur trade,
and habitat destruction have in recent years caused a drastic decline in

the tiger population. No one has reliably calculated how many tigers once inhabited South Asia, but rough estimates [which have fluctuated up and down since the early 1970s] attest to the plight of the cat, which more than any other animal is the symbol of the subcontinent. In that crowded part of the world, where many villages can be found in even the most remote forest tracts, tiger and man will inevitably continue to come into conflict. The only hope for the tiger lies in large, strictly protected reserves.

One very clear reason for the tiger's dilemma, according to P. D. Stracey in his book *Tigers,* lies within the nature of the cat. While the tiger has been an extremely adaptable animal—throughout its long history it has been constantly on the move, crossing most of Asia and accommodating itself to new habitats and climates, till now there are no new places open to it—the tiger is essentially a creature of a closed environment. It must have cover and concealment, and a reasonably steady supply of game species. Obviously, the tiger cannot depend on livestock as a source of food. And the tiger is not a creature of open spaces, not a pack hunter. Even if such habitats were open to it, it is doubtful the species could adjust in time.

Hoping to save the tiger from extinction, the World Wildlife Fund launched "Operation Tiger" in 1973. With the financial assistance of the World Wildlife Fund, several countries have agreed to devote certain areas to tiger conservation. There are nine such areas in India (including Kanha Park), three in Nepal, and one in Bangladesh. I hope that these countries will invite trained wildlife biologists to study the tigers and their prey. To be successful, conservation and management must ultimately depend on knowledge. My study in Kanha Park was a small first step.

Most tigers avoid man so assiduously that it was a rare and joyful occasion when I met one during my wanderings in the forest. Once I found a partially eaten cow hidden in a ravine. The remains had been covered with grass, typical for tiger kills, and I decided to wait nearby for the cat's return. I relaxed with my back resting against a boulder.

Hours later, toward dusk, a leaf rustled behind me. Slowly I raised myself and peered over the rock, straight into the amber eyes of a tigress who stood ten feet away coolly surveying the scene. I recognized her by the facial markings as the mother of the four cubs. Calmly we parted, she retracing her steps, I walking off toward home in the opposite direction, each realizing that the other had intended no harm.

The tiger's relationship to man has been the subject of endless speculation. While the cat obviously fears humans, as most wild creatures do, one must grant it a certain dignity and self-respect in its encounters. It is not in the nature of a tiger to flee or attack immediately when it meets a person—except in those instances when it has been harassed for some time.

Quite often the tiger seems to wish to satisfy its curiosity. At other times, as in the instances I have described, there may be a mutual respect

At Kanha, Kay and our boys, Eric and Mark, occasionally went out by elephant to find tigers.

recognized by both parties. P. D. Stracey describes an incident recounted by A. Locke, about a Malay police sergeant who felt the "kiss of the tiger." Sitting alone on a riverbank at dusk, he was approached by a tiger at such close quarters that he felt its breath on his face. Even though the man was sitting, not standing, which is said to make him a more vulnerable prey to tigers, and it was dusk, the tiger's usual hunting time, the cat simply walked away from him. The incident so impressed the sergeant that he never again would look at a dead tiger and never wanted to help anyone kill one.

The tiger has a reputation for savagery, but this is a myth perpetuated by hunters. When cornered, wounded, or surprised, any tiger may naturally attack in self-defense. The Kanha tigers were remarkably eventempered, readily forgiving an intrusion, as did the tigress on meeting me by her kill. A man-eater, of course, is a different matter. But today only in the Sunderbans—a mangrove swamp at the mouth of the Ganges—are man-eaters fairly common. Hubert Hendrichs, who checked local records during a visit to the area, found that an average of seventy-six people a year were killed there between 1967 and 1971.

Every dawn I searched the forests for the tigress and her cubs, but I seldom found them. At times I discovered one of their kills in a thicket, alerted to its presence by the cawing of scavenging crows, but the family had more often than not departed. Only some bones and stomach contents marked the site of their nocturnal meal. Since an adult tiger can consume over sixty pounds of meat in a few hours, a deer seldom lasts more than a night. Consequently my knowledge of tiger family life in Kanha was based on intermittent glimpses.

So little is known about the life of tigers in the wild that we need far more study before we can speak of the mating and rearing of young in much detail. Females bear young every two and a half to three years on the average. Mated pairs stay together only as long as the female is receptive. One might expect such a large animal to have a long gestation period, but it is only fourteen to fifteen weeks, actually an advantage for a predator that must spend a great deal of time hunting its food.

When the cubs I'd been observing in Kanha Park were about a year old, the tigress found it increasingly difficult to satisfy their voracious appetites. She needed to catch the equivalent of one axis deer a day, but to capture such fleet and alert prey was difficult, and most stalks failed, so she turned to livestock. One night she tore a hole into the wall of our livestock shed and killed a buffalo. Unable to carry it away, she absconded with a lamb which we had been saving for our Christmas dinner.

Lack of food also contributed to the breakup of the family. The male cub, who was considerably larger than his sisters, began to roam alone, always alert for an easy meal. Once, at mid-morning, he suddenly appeared at a village and snatched a domestic pig. The female cubs remained together and, as far as I knew, still depended on their mother.

A tiger can never be sure where its next meal is coming from, so it wastes little, and it must also guard its food supply from scavengers, especially from vultures. Ideally, a tiger will be able to drag its kill to convenient cover, where it will lie up for several hours to several days, until it has consumed the entire food supply. It almost always begins its meal from the rear of the carcass, eating its prey almost completely, including meat, skin, and viscera. Occasionally it will disembowel a carcass, but in Kanha Park the tigers usually consumed the stomach and intestines, though not their contents.

Many accounts have been given of the tiger's method of stalking its prey, not all of them accurate. Most often the cat approaches as closely as possible with the utmost stealth, making incredibly little noise for such a large animal. Then a sudden rush (the tiger is a marvelous sprinter though not much of a long-distance runner) brings it on the animal. Just as it reaches the prey it makes a lunge—usually at the creature's back or side—knocking it over and then quickly grabbing it by the throat, which it holds until the animal suffocates.

When Stan and I observed the family that March, the cubs had taken a further step toward independence. The male cub, who had been hunting by himself off and on for about five months, was now an adept killer, pulling a buffalo down and then holding its throat in a death grip with an efficiency that attested to considerable experience. His sisters also showed skill in overpowering prey. As if aware that her duties toward the cubs had been fulfilled, the tigress now maintained a tenuous contact with her offspring, visiting them only at intervals of several days. Soon the cubs would be fully independent.

My study was at an end. I would never know the fate of these cubs, whether the adult male would evict the young one, whether the female cubs would settle down in the same range as their mother. But I was more than compensated by the knowledge that I had come closer to these wild, mysterious cats than most men . . . closer to unraveling their mystery, not destroying it. And in the process, adding to the store of knowledge desperately needed to secure a place for the tiger in a dramatically changing world.

[1973]

Tracking New Species

Saola

Too often my comments on wildlife species may seem to convey a sense of doom, brief odes to the sunset of life. My research in Laos was different: those days were full of happy anticipation at the prospect of finding something completely unknown. My coworkers and I became old-fashioned explorers, in search not of rare and endangered species but of new ones, or seeking to rediscover creatures that had been lost to science for decades.

In this age of species loss, it is sometimes forgotten that few hoofed animals have become extinct in the past five hundred years. Among these are the aurochs (a progenitor of domestic cattle), the bluebok, Schomburgk's deer, and red gazelle. Yet as recently as the 1990s, the forested Annamite Mountains tracing the border of Laos and Vietnam revealed the spectacular saola, a previously unknown relative of wild oxen, with its striking white facial markings and long black horns. Soon after that, we found a long-missing species of wild pig, discovered the giant barking deer, and rediscovered another type of barking deer. Still a third barking deer—a diminutive one named the Truongson barking deer—was definitely identified through DNA only after I wrote this article. In all, this region yielded three new large mammal species during a single decade, not to mention a new rabbit, a rat, and several bats.

In another case, an animal discussed in this chapter proved not to exist: the linh duong. Its horns, which two German biologists used as a basis to describe a new genus and species, were shown to be fake—locally manufactured from cow horn by heating, twisting, and grinding. No matter: science ultimately *corrects itself. The saola's sudden emergence from the forest's shadows, however, has given great impetus to conservation of the Annamite Mountains. Both Laos and Vietnam are proud of this unique and elusive creature, found only in their two countries.*

We follow three Hmong tribesmen along a barely discernible trail that traces ridge crests and angles up and down steep slopes. The dense rainforest canopy seals off the sky, leaving the undergrowth of saplings, bamboos, and palms in gloom. It is drizzling, as it does much of the time high in the Annamite Mountains of Laos bordering Vietnam. We continuously glance around, hoping to glimpse a saola in the shadows.

The saola, a species of large mammal unknown to science until 1992, was described in nearby Vietnam by biologists Do Tuoc and John MacKinnon after they found several sets of horns in villages. It was the first of an astonishing and marvelous assemblage of new mammals that has come to light in the remote and biologically unique Annamites. During the 1990s, in fact, more species of hoofed animals have been discovered or rediscovered here alone than are known to have become extinct worldwide in the past few hundred years. No one except a handful of villagers in the region, however, has ever seen a live saola in the wild.

I am here in this extraordinary biological hot spot on my first of four visits between 1994 and 1997, conducting wildlife surveys in a cooperative venture of New York's Wildlife Conservation Society (WCS) and the Lao Forest Department. My associate, biologist Alan Rabinowitz, and his wife, Salisa, are along, as are several Laotian colleagues. In addition to finding saola and other creatures, known and unknown, our long-range intent is to help find a way to preserve these magnificent forests and their wildlife. But for now the only wildlife we see are land leeches humping expectantly toward us over the moldering leaves on the forest floor.

Hmong villagers hold up the horns of two saola. The meat was eaten or sold at a market. These photos were taken in the Annamite Mountains of Laos, near the border of Vietnam.

The chance of finding new species of large mammals adds a special aura of excitement and anachronistic pleasure to our wildlife surveys. After all, only a few such species have been found this century: okapi, giant forest hog, mountain nyala, Chacoan peccary, bonobo, kouprey. I feel like a nineteenth-century biologist but with a difference. Discoveries, I soon learn, are made not in the depths of the forest but in village huts and markets. Wildlife is so intensively hunted with guns, deadfalls, and snares that signs or sightings of any mammals are uncommon.

Two days earlier we were told that saola meat had been for sale in a market in Lak Xao, a small town at the foot of the Annamites. The news of a saola, even a dead one, naturally arouses our intense interest. Vendors at the market direct us to the Hmong village of Nape. There our inquiries about saola are at first treated with suspicion. After all, Laotians have had mainly unpleasant experiences with Americans. During the Vietnam War, neutral Laos was pounded with rockets and bombs, partly in a futile attempt to disrupt the Ho Chi Minh Trail, that

Villages in the Annamites are isolated, often a day's walk apart. We made monthlong treks on foot and followed rivers by dugout in search of wildlife. Animals are scarce, since they are hunted intensively for food; the best way to find out where certain mammals occur is to inquire at villages and search the markets.

shifting network of forest paths and roads over which North Vietnam moved military equipment southward. Now the Hmong had different worries. "Are you sure they are not DEA [Drug Enforcement Agency]?" asks one of another. Finally convinced that we are only interested in wildlife, they bring us two sets of saola horns, one still rank.

I move my fingers along the smooth, black surface of one horn, marveling at its rarity and elegance. Slightly curved, the horns are fifty centimeters (twenty inches) long. They resemble those of the African oryx antelope, the basis for the animal's scientific name *Pseudoryx*, or "false oryx." The local name *saola* means "spindle horn": the horns resemble the upright posts of the spindles used in local weaving. How could a ninety-kilogram (two-hundred-pound) animal with such magnificent horns elude scientific detection for so long, even though war and revolution have hampered research in the Annamites for half a century?

"We'll catch you a live one," says a Hmong, seeing our lively curiosity. "But what will you give us?" We assure the crowd that has pressed into the room that we only want to study the animal in the wild. Several Hmong agree to take us to the site where they had killed a saola a few days before.

We follow them through the forests, to the headwaters of a stream at an elevation of about 1,700 meters (5,500 feet). Dogs had chased the saola, a female, until here among moss-covered boulders she had made her last stand. As she faced the dogs with her rapier horns, the men came close and shot her. Her hide is still here, chestnut and black in color with splotches of white on the face and a streak of white on the rump. By the ashes of a fire, where the Hmong had butchered and eaten part of her, are hooves shaped like a miniature cow's.

The saola is so strikingly unique that biologists at first found it difficult to pinpoint its closest relatives. One concluded that it belongs with the sheep and goats, another that it resembles the nilgai antelope of India. Detailed DNA analyses, conducted by John Gatesy of the University of Arizona, finally showed that the saola is allied to wild cattle and buffalo. Subsequent surveys by myself and others from WCS, as well as teams in Vietnam, found that saola today are mainly confined to the high and wet parts of the Annamites. Their distribution is patchy, scattered within about 5,200 square kilometers (2,000 square miles), and their number is low, perhaps a few hundred. This makes them highly vulnerable to hunting and to the destruction of the mature rainforest, which they prefer.

During this and other trips, my local team and I often walk for days through the mountains. On this visit, after hours of traversing forest, we come, as we typically do, to a clearing with grass-thatched huts and fields planted with upland rice. Laotians are polite and hospitable people. The headman invites us into his hut, where we sit on floor mats, drink tea, and tell him of the purpose of our visit. The whole village gathers to listen and watch.

We inquire about and show pictures of tiger, clouded leopard, elephant, gaur, sun bear, sambar deer, and others. But what new species might be here to discover? My eyes scan the walls searching for antlers

A private menagerie had an unusual muntjac, or barking deer, and we recognized it as a new species, the giant barking deer. Its horns are widely found in village huts, used as hat and coat racks.

and horns that are often used as clothes racks. Most trophies are of red barking deer, or muntjac, a solitary species the size of a Labrador retriever. Widespread in the tropics of Asia, the red barking deer (and other barking deer species too) is so named because the animals bark like small dogs when excited. They have spiked antlers, often hooked at the tip, about ten to thirteen centimeters (four to five inches) long.

I occasionally see and measure sets of muntjac antlers that are unusually robust and long, about twenty-three centimeters (nine inches). However, it is not until I encounter a live male in a private menagerie in Lak Xao that various unusual features of this deer become obvious. Others of our team also examine this deer and note its large size, short and broad tail, grizzled gray-brown coat, and other characteristics that do not match those of the red muntjac. It is a new species, the giant muntjac, soon thereafter also discovered in Vietnam. Actually it has a wide distribution in the Annamites, as well as southward into Cambodia. Its existence was known as far back as 1899—a photo of its antlers was published in a scientific journal—but it was not recognized as new.

During my village interviews, I always ask about the saola, giant barking deer, and other species. For the saola, the answer is usually no or none now. For the giant barking deer, the answer is often positive: some had been seen in the tall forest beyond, or someone had a set of antlers, but it had been sold to the Vietnamese, who use them in traditional medicines. Several times, I am also told of a small, black barking deer. Very rare. Its name is *fan dong*, "barking deer of mature forest." No one has any skulls of this elusive creature: animals are quickly eaten and the bones recycled by dogs and pigs.

In January 1995, WCS's William Robichaud and Rob Timmins among others, including myself, visit the Lak Xao menagerie again. And there we find a diminutive black muntjac with a bright orange cap and antlers less than an inch long. It looks like a new species. But is it? In 1929 one specimen of a similar muntjac was collected far away in northern Laos and given the species name *rooseveltorum* in honor of one of President Theodore Roosevelt's sons who led the expedition. Ultimately we would obtain some skulls. George Amato of WCS would compare their DNA with that of the *rooseveltorum* specimen and find that it was probably the same. Rather than adding a new species, we may have rediscovered one that had vanished for six decades.

Wildlife information from villages such as Lak Xao has to be carefully evaluated: the local concept of a species is not necessarily the same as mine, and fact and fiction sometimes become interwoven. But I am intrigued to hear of two kinds of wild pig in one area. Only one was known from the Annamites, the common black Eurasian pig. The other was said to be yellowish and long-snouted. In 1892, a Jesuit priest in Shanghai, Fr. Pierre-Marie Heude, had obtained two skulls from southern Vietnam and described these as a new species of pig. Nothing more was heard of the creature, and it was thought to be extinct, if it had existed at all. For more than a month I hike through the Annamites, climbing ridge after ridge and descending turbulent rivers by dugout together with my coworkers William Leacock and Khamkhoun Khounboline. Again and again, we ask about the yellow pig. Finally in one hut we find half a head and a leg being smoke-dried over the open hearth. I am told that this is what is left of a yellow pig. We buy and eat the remains but save the bones. Measurements by Colin Groves of Australian National University and DNA analysis by George Amato show that it is indeed the missing pig species, resurrected after a century.

Near the southern tip of the Annamites, in Vietnam and Cambodia, is the home of a mystery creature. The local Vietnamese call it *linh duong*, "mountain goat." Its horns are up to fifty-one centimeters (twenty inches) long, spiral-shaped with a curl at the tip, and there are ringlike ridges along the entire length. Only the horns have been found so far; no one is sure what the animal looks like or even which are its closest relatives. I could find no evidence of it in Laos. A Chinese encyclopedia, the *San Cai Tu Hui,* dated 1607, shows a goatlike creature with curly horns that might be the *linh duong*. The animal is probably close to extinction, being even rarer than the kouprey, the huge forest ox that was discovered in the same region in 1936.

Local people brought this pregnant female saola into town, where she soon died.
PHOTO BY ALAN RABINOWITZ, USED WITH HIS PERMISSION.

The Annamites present a living lost world, a place about which little is as yet known, and one can only speculate about why the region has such a unique assemblage of species. During the Pleistocene Epoch, the world's climate oscillated between wet and warmer phases and cooler and drier ones, as with each ice age the glaciers advanced and retreated. Such changes affected the distribution of rainforest upon which such species as the saola and several barking deer depend. During a dry phase, suitable forest persisted mainly high in the Annamites. And there certain species survived and others evolved in isolation, a Noah's Ark lost in time.

During the height of the last glacial period, about 18,000 years ago, sea levels were lower. Islands such as Sumatra, Borneo, and Java were then part of the Indochinese mainland. Some Annamite species have their closest relatives far to the south or even on the Indonesian islands, thereby revealing their ancient lineage. For example, the rediscovered pig has its only relatives, the warty pigs, on these islands. In 1996, biologist Rob Timmins found a short-eared, zebra-striped rabbit in the Lak Xao market. It is unique to mainland Asia, but a similarly striped rabbit lives on Sumatra. The crested argus pheasant is found in the Annamites and also far away on the Malay Peninsula.

The new discoveries have drawn attention to the Annamites just in time. Large tracts of old-growth rainforest have already been cut by the slash-and-burn cultivators who use a field for a year or two, after which they leave it fallow, the soil exhausted, while they cut new forest. Commercial logging has an ever-increasing impact, removing the stately forests upon which so many species—from gibbons and hornbills to saola—depend. Logging and the construction of dams promote an influx of people, and new roads enable settlers and hunters to penetrate easily into remote areas.

Actually, the discovery of the saola has increased hunting pressure on the species because local people are now aware of a market for specimens and live animals. In Vietnam's Vu Quang Nature Reserve, where the saola was discovered and the Swiss-based World Wide Fund for Nature had a field station, twenty-one saola were killed and three were removed alive to Hanoi between 1992 and 1994. In Laos the Hmong caught seven saola, but only one, a female, reached Lak Xao alive, where she survived three weeks. She was pregnant. William Robichaud saw her there and was enchanted. She readily permitted herself to be hand-fed and stroked. To the Hmong, the saola is *saht supahp,* "the polite animal," because of its placid nature.

Fortunately Laos and Vietnam have established several reserves and conservation areas in the Annamites. The two countries are also holding meetings in a cooperative attempt to save this biological treasure from the past. All existing and proposed reserves contain villages. But if properly managed in cooperation with the local people, they can offer the forests and its inhabitants a future. In 1812, the French naturalist Georges Cuvier wrote that "there is little hope of discovering new species of large quadrupeds." The saola and others proved his prediction wrong. Indeed, another potentially new species of barking deer has recently emerged from the Annamites, and the forest's shadows may still shroud other mystery creatures.

[1998]

166

Chinese Treasures

Golden Monkey and Takin

The giant panda is famous, a wonder of creation, and the attention devoted to it also benefits thousands of other plant and animal species that inhabit the same mountain forests. Two such creatures are the golden monkey and the takin, both golden in color and endangered—one beautiful and the other perhaps best described as unique. But everything exists in its own perfection.

I observed both of these animals casually while wandering through forests in search of pandas. The takin still awaits an interpreter to provide a legacy of its existence, though Chinese biologists have added some information about its natural history. The golden monkeys in China are now considered three separate species, rather than just subspecies, of which the one I encountered in Sichuan is the most widespread and abundant with an estimated 15,000 individuals surviving. (The Guizhou golden monkey numbers only about 800 animals and the Yunnan species 1,500.) When I watched them, I had no idea about how the large monkey groups were organized socially. Chinese researchers have now studied the species intensively and shown that each group is divided into subgroups composed of one male with his harem of females and their youngsters; in addition, males without harems may form their own subgroup. This social system, rare in primates, is also found in the hamadryas and gelada baboons of Ethiopia.

The bamboo thickets are rigid with frost, rhododendron leaves have curled tightly for the winter, and fir boughs sag with snow. The mountains are silent in the January cold, the crunch of my boots on snow the only sound. I am in China's Wolong Nature Reserve, trudging along the spine of a ridge at 10,300 feet in search of fresh giant panda tracks. Ahead of me, a branch snaps and crashes through the tree canopy, then another. Cautiously, I move toward the sound. Golden monkeys. A male at the periphery of the scattered group spots me. After an intent look, he emits several chucking calls, like an agitated blackbird, and leaps wildly downslope, golden mantle of hair trailing as he hurls his 35-pound body from tree to tree. The others, startled by his sudden flight, follow.

Golden hair on shoulders and back, a white belly, dark cap, and a gray tail tipped with white make *Rhinopithecus roxellanae* one of the handsomest of all monkeys. Its nose tips jauntily upward. In fact, when the French scientist Alphonse Milne-Edwards first described the species in 1870, he named it with quirky humor after Roxellana, the beautiful mistress of a Turkish sultan whose charms included a snub nose. This probably is the main feature they shared, for the golden monkey also has a bright blue face, and the male has a wart in each corner of its upper lip. Living in an area where most large mammals—musk deer, tufted deer, black bear, and others—have cryptic, concealing colors, the golden monkey is an exuberant exception.

During my wanderings through Sichuan's forests, I saw a group of the animals occasionally, but their shyness permitted only brief observations. Still, these encounters with a largely unstudied big primate were enough to intrigue me. Golden monkeys live in an environment perhaps more severe than that experienced by any other monkey. Throughout the snowbound winter they remain at high elevations in temperate forests. How do they survive winter?

Winter is not the only danger golden monkeys have faced. The monkey's striking fur was once highly prized. During the Qing Dynasty (1644–1911) clothing made of golden monkey skins was an indication

A male golden monkey struts along a branch, tail arched, showing his dominance. These monkeys search the snow-covered boughs for a meager winter diet of lichens.

of high status. Because of its value, the monkeys were extensively killed. At the same time, their mountainous habitat was disappearing as demand for timber increased and agriculturists pushed fields ever higher up the hillsides. Because of these factors, the species has been so decimated that it now survives as three species in only three limited areas in China.

The species I observed in Wolong has its fate tied to the giant panda, for the two share almost identical ranges along the eastern edge of the Tibetan Plateau. No reliable estimates of numbers exist. But, like the panda, the monkeys prefer forests above 6,500 feet, a habitat that is now fragmented and often confined to isolated mountaintops. However, several populations are protected in reserves, including those of Wolong in the Qionglai Mountains and Tangjiahe in the Min Mountains. Fortunately, the Chinese government prizes the golden monkey so highly that it has given the animal complete protection, ranking it with the panda as a national treasure. Outside of China, only the San Diego Zoo has been able to obtain animals.

Golden monkeys are basically leaf-eaters, related to the langur and colobus. For much of the year they stuff themselves on leaves of birch, wild cherry, maple, and other trees. They readily forage on the ground too, eating, for example, wild onions. But in the winter bare forest, there are few leaves. The monkeys' main winter diet, I was surprised to note, consists of several kinds of lichens, which in this humid climate thrive on tree trunks and branches. The animals clamber and leap through the trees with great agility, plucking lichens rapidly either by hand or directly by mouth. Choice morsels often grow on dead branches, and rather than risk a tumble, a monkey will break off the branch, hold it in one hand, and eat leisurely.

A group of golden monkeys needs a constant, large winter supply of lichens. But lichens grow slowly. Once stripped, a tree probably requires many years before its boughs will support a new harvest. This may be one reason why a group's range is large—exceptionally large for an arboreal monkey. I spent many months in a ten-square-mile valley. Sometimes I neither heard nor saw a monkey for weeks. Then suddenly a group returned, and the quiet valley filled with noise as branches cracked and animals emitted the peculiar nasal whine by which group members maintain contact. Just as suddenly, they vanished into distant valleys where our panda-tracking work seldom took us. The forest seemed lonely without them.

Three groups, each containing sixty to seventy-five individuals, visited our valley one winter. It is difficult to count groups precisely because foraging animals may be spread over a quarter mile of forest. In April, however, when spring leaves provide unlimited food again, a dramatic change occurs in the social life of the golden monkey of Wolong: several groups in an area join and travel together as one supergroup. They stay together until about October, at which time the approaching winter dictates a smaller group size for efficient foraging. About 200 to 250 monkeys had congregated into one supergroup in our valley. When it appeared on a slope, the forest canopy swayed and the hills resounded to the cries of the golden horde. Groups with more than 500 golden monkeys have been reported, an extraordinary figure for any primate except humans.

One morning I met a group resting peacefully in sun that had just descended the winter slope. Seven juveniles clambered playfully together among the boughs of a spruce, and a number of females sat nearby in another tree. A large male swaggered along a branch, his tail looped in a dominant arc, and approached one of the females with an infant at her chest and a juvenile by her side. Tenderly he groomed the juvenile. Then, going to another female with an infant, he tried to groom that youngster, too, but its mother enveloped it in her arms. Forcefully, he yanked the infant from her, groomed it gently, and released it back to its mother's embrace.

The golden monkey remains unstudied, its biography unwritten. As my fleeting glimpses of it show, the animal promises a treasure of information to whoever is the first to uncover its secrets. In the meantime, golden monkeys fill the mind, seize the imagination. Their footprints in the snow, resembling those of a barefoot infant, inspire admiration for the monkeys' determined disregard of the elements. Their matchless beauty among the birch boughs creates concern as they leap toward an uncertain destiny.

What creature has the bulky humped body of a brown bear, the sloping hindquarters of a spotted hyena, the legs of a cow, the broad flat tail of a goat, the knobby horns of a wildebeest, and the face of a moose with mumps? The takin, of course. If, as has been said, the camel resembles an animal designed by committee, then the takin looks like an animal assembled by the same committee from spare parts.

Although a takin may weigh 650 pounds and stand fifty inches high at the shoulder, only connoisseurs of the exotic have heard of it. Prepare a list of large hoofed mammals with obscure names—eland, kudu, tapir, topi, nilgai, gaur, takin—and the takin is the least likely to evoke

Bull takins were at times quite tolerant of me watching them browse to determine their food habits. The Sichuan takin is a mottled tan and black, in contrast to a subspecies in the eastern Himalaya that is mostly brown and one in the Qinling Mountains of China that is golden.

an image. Yet *Budorcas taxicolor* deserves recognition, for it is an impressive creature.

In addition to its peculiar appearance, it comes in three basic color models. In the western part of its range, from Bhutan eastward along the slopes of the Himalaya to Burma and into China, the animal is dark brown. Farther east, mainly along the edge of the Tibetan Plateau in China's Sichuan Province, it is straw-colored with splotches of gray-black on legs, flanks, back, and rump. And in the Qinling Mountains of China's Shaanxi Province, it is golden.

The remoteness of these regions, penetrated by few Westerners even early in the twentieth century, when political borders were more permeable—has assured the takin its privacy. And so has its habitat. Takins prefer rugged mountains above 4,000 feet, where they lead a shadowed life in forests, thickets, and dense bamboo. Occasionally animals ascend to timberline, at about 12,000 feet, and graze at the edges of alpine meadows.

I became familiar with takins while studying giant pandas in 1984 in the Min Mountains of northern Sichuan. There, in the Tangjiahe Nature Reserve, signs of takins are pervasive. Any hike through the mountain forests of conifer and birch follows takin trails, for the animals consistently select the best routes around cliffs and along ridges. In valleys, the willow stands where a herd has foraged often look as if hit by a small hurricane. A strong barnyard odor, or perhaps even the thumps of fleeing hooves, may speak of a nearby beast, but the forest hides its inhabitants well.

Many hillsides in Tangjiahe were logged and cultivated ten years ago, and they are now overgrown with brambles and saplings. Bulls like to forage there, generally alone but sometimes in twos or threes, remaining in a favorite patch for days. At times I would meet a lone bull resting massive and still like a boulder. On sensing my presence he would rise to face me—motionless, head high, nostrils flared, brown eyes scrutinizing me over his curved black muzzle. Usually he would bolt, tearing up vines and shrubs by the roots in his crashing retreat. But if he abruptly lowered his horns and snorted in threat, I prudently conceded right of way; misanthropic bulls have been known to attack and gore the unwary.

Predictably, in the early morning and late afternoon I could observe them foraging, ponderous and placid like domestic cows. Takins are not, however, allied to cattle but to sheep and goats; their closest living relative is the Arctic musk ox.

Like the proverbial goats, takins eat almost any plant within reach of their broad mouths; I casually tallied well more than a hundred food species. In winter and early spring, the animals often browse on bamboo leaves and the leathery leaves of evergreen rhododendrons and oaks; gnaw and strip bark off young pines, willows, and wild cherries; and clip horsetails that protrude from the snow. Their size and strength enable them to reach morsels denied to tufted deer and musk deer, serow, and other hoofed animals with whom they share the mountains. Rearing up, a takin can balance on its hind legs to nip off branch tips eight feet above ground. Or, less delicately, it may prop its forelegs or just its chest against a tree trunk and then lean forward until the tree snaps. If a stem merely bends under the weight, the takin straddles it to keep it from springing erect while leisurely browsing; it may push over trees up to five inches in diameter in this way.

In spite of their skill in demolishing trees, winter is a lean period for takins. One March day, I met a bull whose hindquarters were just bone encased in taut hide, his spine serrated like a dragon's. He tottered down-valley feeding on dry sage leaves. After crossing a stream, he stumbled and fell, and too weak to rise, he died at the water's edge. He was old, his cheek teeth worn flat, his weight only 458 pounds. Adult takins in Sichuan have no natural predators except perhaps the pack-hunting dhole (Asia's wild dog), and most are born to leave life calmly, not to lose it.

Finally, by late April, succulent greens carpet the lower slopes, and saplings and shrubs are in tender leaf. Takins gorge on this nutritious new growth—the leaves of hydrangea, viburnum, poplar, bramble, wild rose, and maple, as well as such herbs as primrose, anemone, nettle, aster, wild parsnip, thistle, sour dock, and buttercup, to name just a few.

Unlike solitary bulls, females and their offspring tend to spend most of the year high on forested slopes. More than a hundred of them traversed the mountains around our camp, usually in herds of from fifteen to thirty-five animals, including one or more bulls as hangers-on. But by early May, after the April calving season, several of the herds had apparently joined for a while and, attracted by the spring growth, descended into the valleys together.

One day when the peaks stood sharp-edged against blue sky and the slopes shimmered with soft green, I observed a herd of about a hundred animals as they left the forest for a clearing. Several young bulls and yearlings with spiked horns came bucking and bounding; infected by such frisky spirits, females leaped sedately. Though weighing a third less

Takins like to stand broadside to the sun to warm up during cold winter days. This bull liked to linger near our camp, and we named him Lao Pengyou, Old Friend.

than bulls, females have the same sturdy body—designed for plodding over precipitous terrain, not for kicking up heels—and their efforts lacked a certain grace. It puzzled me to see no young. But then they came, all together—a tumble of takins, dark brown and fuzzy—gamboling after one female. Young spend many hours of the day in a kindergarten tended by one babysitter, while their mothers forage and socialize. One female had sixteen youngsters in tow.

Herds as well as bulls climbed the slopes as summer approached, and we seldom saw them in the valleys from late May until they descended again with autumn in October. Around August, bulls gave up their solitary ways to join females for the rut. Hidden by swirling rain clouds that engulf the mountains in that season, takins have so far concealed this part of their life from scientific voyeurs. I can, however, visualize bulls competing for a cow in heat, for I have observed their strife in other contexts.

Like males of many species, takin bulls prefer to intimidate an opponent rather than waste energy and risk injury in an actual fight.

With a stiff arthritic gait and with neck arched so far down that the muzzle is almost between the forelegs, one bull cuts slowly broadside in front of the other, looking as if utterly weary. The posture, however, displays his massive body to full advantage; it is designed to impress. If the other bull does not turn away, or at least signal submission by feeding intently with seeming lack of concern, the threatening animal may sidle closer, growling and grunting.

Two evenly matched opponents may display to each other in this humped posture, walking parallel about six feet apart. Then, if neither gives way, horn meets horn and a sparring match decides matters. With short curved horns locked, the bulls shove, bodies straining. One may break away to scramble up the slope, for whichever animal attains an uphill position adds the force of gravity to his attack; the bull below, knowing he will be driven downhill, rushes in, and the other, to protect his flank, turns to lock horns once more. And so the quest for dominance continues—whirling, chasing, hooking, pushing.

Unlike many rare and little-known species that are silently vanishing because no one speaks in their behalf, China's takins have friends in high places. The government considers the takin a precious animal, in the same category as the giant panda and the golden monkey, and has provided it with full protection. Given a reprieve from the shooting and snaring of the past, takins have in recent years increased, according to surveys made under the auspices of China's Ministry of Forestry.

At least 1,300 golden takins survive in the Qinling Mountains; and probably several thousand Sichuan takins roam the Min, Qionglai, and other mountains. The golden and the Sichuan takins often share habitat with giant pandas, much to their advantage: twelve reserves have been established for pandas, and these simultaneously protect takins and their forests from the continuing threat of agriculturists who extend their plantings of maize, potatoes, and beans ever higher up the hillsides. Two other reserves—the Labahe, in northern Sichuan, and the Tsashui, in Shaanxi—were created mainly for takins.

Although takins are relatively numerous, it is difficult to make their acquaintance. Most of the animals' domain is off limits to casual travelers. And China has not permitted its takins to emigrate to foreign zoos; the species is rare even in Chinese zoos. For those who have an unappeasable urge to gaze upon the phlegmatic countenance of a living takin, even a captive one, there are just two choices outside China. The takins to which I refer are of the dark brown Burmese variety. The Bronx Zoo at one time had three of them, but they never bred successfully and two were loaned to the Catskill Game Farm, in upper New York State, where one survives; the zoo in East Berlin also exhibits them.

Although the takin and the giant panda share a home and each in its own way is uniquely beautiful, the takin will never receive the same adulation the panda does; perhaps the best it can hope for is a stray appearance in crossword puzzles. But no matter. For those who know the takin or who treasure wildlife, it is enough that this animal continues to thrive in its mist-shrouded mountain forests.

[1985]

Bound to Bamboo

Giant Panda

In 1981, Kay and I moved into a tent in the Wolong Nature Reserve to study giant pandas on behalf of World Wildlife Fund and in cooperation with Chinese biologists. The project began with a headlong passion for a grand cause: saving a national treasure and a symbol of world conservation. Any such project combines science, economics, and politics, and given the panda's unique status, it seemed at times that research had a low priority. Nevertheless, knowledge about a species is essential before one can protect and manage it effectively.

When we left Wolong in 1985, we had completed the first detailed field study, and more important, conservation was now high on China's agenda in spite of some disillusioning problems. For example, between 1975 and 1989 pandas lost half of their habitat to logging and agriculture. It was thought that perhaps no more than one thousand pandas remained, in twenty-four isolated forest patches.

By 1989, however, a management plan for the panda had been written, one that included forest protection, human land use, and community development. More reserves were soon added to the original thirteen, and they now number forty, covering more than half of the panda's habitat and benefiting the takin, golden monkey, and other species as well. Local staff has been trained in patrolling reserves to reduce poaching and in monitoring panda numbers. A fifteen-year study by Chinese scientists in the Qinling Mountains, beginning in 1985, has greatly advanced our understanding of the species. And a logging ban instituted in 1998 protects not only pandas but also the watersheds upon which *the livelihood of local people depends. A recent census, the first thorough one, places panda numbers at about 1,600.*

Pride, ethics, beauty, and economic incentives, such as tourism and loans of pandas to zoos, have combined to offer hope for the species, so fettered by bamboo and so vulnerable as a result. But, as I wrote in a report, "The panda is not safe. Nor will it ever be. It will always be threatened by something, attracting adversity as readily as adoration. We know what the panda needs: a forest with bamboo, a den for its young, and freedom from persecution. . . . To protect this luminous fragment of life means that we must monitor its fate with vigilance, compassion, wisdom, and loyalty, with a commitment measured in terms not of decades but of centuries."

For many years the female panda has roamed the remote Zhou Shui valley in China's Wolong Nature Reserve. She usually remains high on the slopes, above 9,000 feet, where, in the cold clammy air, arrow bamboo thrives beneath a canopy of lofty firs. Once a year, however, in May and June, she descends below 8,000 feet to feast on the thick juicy shoots of umbrella bamboo that grow at that altitude. The forest has guarded her with its seclusion, and she has probably made her annual trek unseen on shadowed pathways at least a dozen times. She has now grown elderly. Several teeth on the left side of her lower jaw are missing, her canines are yellowed and blunted, and her hip bones are sharp beneath a woolly hide. She weighs 190 pounds.

I know these intimate facts about her because on March 13, 1981, she entered one of our live traps. As part of a collaborative China/World Wildlife Fund program to study the giant panda, we have so far collared five animals with radio transmitters in order to be able to trace movements and monitor activity.

After sedating the panda, Howard Quigley, a research fellow of the New York Zoological Society, fastened a radio collar around her neck while Hu Jinchu, Pan Wenshi, Wang Lianke, and other Chinese team

A female panda, whom we named Zhen-Zhen (meaning "precious"), walks through her typical bamboo habitat in the Wolong Nature Reserve.

members checked her for ectoparasites and helped measure and weigh her. Later, fully recovered from the tranquilizing drug, she returned to the obscurity of the forest. We named her Zhen-Zhen, meaning "precious or rare treasure."

Eating a swath through her domain, she travels little, sometimes no more than 200 yards in a day. But when the bamboo shoots sprout in May, she descends to search for them assiduously, so much so that almost every thicket contains signs of her passing: small piles of sheaths, or bamboo casings, and other debris where she tarried briefly to consume a shoot or two. Shoots are nutritious—no doubt one reason she favors them after a long, lean winter—but they also consist of about 90 percent water. To subsist on shoots, she must eat prodigious amounts:

we calculated that she may stuff herself with six hundred shoots, weighing sixty-six pounds or more, in a day.

Although Zhen-Zhen's radio signal always reveals her location, she only once allowed us to observe her in the two months that followed her capture and release.

One afternoon in May, I follow the contours of a mountainside, engaged in what can be considered the romantic misery of fieldwork—searching through sodden thickets for panda droppings to analyze their content, radio-locating pandas by triangulation while glacial fog chills the body, doing all the prosaic tasks by which a scientific account is ultimately measured. Most field biologists wander the wilderness, leading a free but lonely life, not, I suppose, to enhance academic credentials or seek rewards, but for the love of such work, as well as the touch of romance that even a project barren of adventure can provide.

I halt on a rise, assemble my portable antenna, and tune the radio receiver to 194, Zhen-Zhen's frequency. The signal is so insistent that I glance around, almost expecting her to emerge from the undergrowth; she is just downhill of me. I find a small clearing and wait there, sitting silently among ferns.

Immobile clouds hang low in the valley, their escape arrested by the surrounding ridges that climb higher and higher like dragons' spines. Great spruce and hemlock boughs sag from incessant rain, the leaves of rhododendrons droop, and bamboo stems stand in dark closed ranks against outsiders; even the still air seems weighed down with melancholy. Then a sound transforms the forest—the snap of a bamboo shoot breaking, soon followed by the rustle of sheaths being pulled from the shoot, and finally by loud crunching as a panda eats the tender center. My eyes try to penetrate the bamboo but see only various shades of blackness, belonging to moss-covered rocks and trunks of trees. My vigil continues, the forest now without stir or sound.

A fleeting movement behind a thin screen of bamboo: Zhen-Zhen has angled noiselessly uphill on padded paws, and I see her sitting down, hunched, her bowed legs extended in front of her. She leans sideways to grasp the top of a bamboo shoot with one hand and with the same motion bites and snaps off the shoot near its base. After that she settles back, peeling and chomping, the shoot disappearing within a minute. Glancing around, she spies another and just as adroitly consumes it, her actions hushed and deliberate, in complete accord with her surroundings.

There is a magic monotony to a panda's existence, revolving, as it does, wholly around bamboo. The unbounded bamboo slopes provide the panda with safety and peace as well as food. The animal is literally engulfed by food, bamboo stems and leaves crowding in on all sides and from above—a twilight environment almost subterranean in quality.

Evolution provided the panda with special adaptations for subsisting in a bamboo habitat: a prehensile elongate wrist bone—a sixth finger, which functions as a thumb for handling bamboo stems—and broad flat molars for crushing them. Sometimes a panda will eat other plants, such as wild parsnip, and it relishes meat on the rare occasions when some can be found, perhaps at an abandoned leopard kill. However, bamboo is the essential component of the animal's existence. Because of the plant's constant availability, even during winter, the panda has forgone hibernation and, unlike bears, single-mindedly continues foraging through the season of snows.

Evolution has delivered the panda from options. Freed from choices, it seems more free than most animals. But, in fact, bamboo has robbed the panda of innovative vigor, imprisoning it with an ecological possessiveness that knows no alternative. Nothing else exists for the panda: the animal is fettered by the bamboo's impassive power.

Pandas lived in much of eastern China and south into Burma during the Pleistocene but apparently vanished from much of this range when a change to a drier climate eliminated bamboo. An expanding human population evicted the panda from many of its last refuges, until now perhaps only a thousand survive in the mountains along the eastern rim of the Tibetan Plateau. The Chinese government has established twelve reserves to protect these remnants, Wolong being the largest with an area of 800 square miles.

A panda in the Tangjiahe Nature Reserve peers at us from a pine tree after we disturbed its midday rest there.

Still, pandas are tied to the fate of bamboo. Certain bamboo species flower and die at intervals of sixty to one hundred years or more, nearly all plants in an area bursting into bloom and then perishing at about the same time. Such mass death of a food source can lead to the pandas' starvation unless other bamboo species are available as food.

Agriculturists have increasingly eliminated such alternate species as they have pushed their fields ever farther up valleys and steep hillsides, leaving only mountaintops capped with bamboo. When between 1974 and 1976 umbrella bamboo died throughout an area of more than two thousand square miles in the pandas' northern range, so did nearly 140 pandas. Rather than marvel at Zhen-Zhen's evolutionary specializations, I am touched by the tragic history of her race, her helplessness. Indifferent fates have mastered her, and now only man still needs her, as a symbol of his loyalty to the Earth.

Zhen-Zhen raises her nose, seeming to test the air. I think she has sensed my presence. With a rolling motion she rises and steps from behind the bamboo into a bower from which a path leads to my clearing. Now, for the first time, her ill-defined shape evolves fully into a panda. She ambles toward me with a combination of shyness and audacity, her round white head bright in the dark foliage, like a full moon on a frosty night. Her black legs and ears dissolve into the shadows to create an illusion of a luminous silver creature floating glowing and ghostlike toward me. She advances to within 35 feet, then stops to bob her huge head up and down and snort softly to herself.

My anxious eyes look for some shade of expression in her face, an intimation of her coming actions, but it remains inert, with a Buddha-like complacency showing neither passion nor gentleness. There are two pandas, the one in the mind and the other in its wilderness home. Soft, furry, and wide-eyed, with a large round head and a flat face, a panda in captivity is usually viewed as the ultimate toy, something to cuddle and play with. But here, among the towering spruce, the panda is imposing, monumental in its lonely greatness, inviting neither familiarity nor fear, complete in itself, preordained, final.

After an intense gaze in my direction, Zhen-Zhen retreats to the margin of the bamboo. She sits there in repose, bleating gently in agitation. It is a strangely moving sound. Her bleats grow softer and stop as her head sags onto her chest. The slow rhythmic heaving of her bulky body reveals a peculiar fact: imperturbably, she has fallen asleep.

A panda spends some ten to sixteen hours a day or more eating—in daytime as well as night—interspersing periods of foraging with rest and sleep. Although Zhen-Zhen has just eaten, I hardly expected her to doze off in front of me. Is there imagination in that broad hard skull? Has she no resources except her desperate desire to lead a solitary life and recycle bamboo? Zhen-Zhen and I are together yet hopelessly separated by an immense space. Her aspirations remain impenetrable, her behavior inscrutable; I am not even certain what questions to ask of her.

She awakes after a while and without hesitation moves away, silently drawing the shadows of the bamboo around her so abruptly that her dissolution is startling.

I remain until fog turns the trees into intangible forms and a soft rain whispers among the leaves. How long I have been in the clearing is uncertain; time has no single measure. Absorbed in the panda, I am released from past and future until her departure breaks the spell of our meeting, leaving me with feelings stronger than any memory; I seem to have retained little beyond the luminous fact of Zhen-Zhen's existence. But perhaps that is enough. There is a Buddhist instruction that urges man to listen to the farthest sound. For a long time I have sought that which is hidden and most elusive, and for a shining moment I may have been near it on this mist-shrouded mountain.

[1983]

Author's note: *What follows are excerpts from an article titled "Notes of a Professional Panda-Watcher," which reprinted my monthly letters written to the Wildlife Conservation Society and the World Wildlife Fund during the panda radio-tracking project. They offer details on our observations and on life in the Wolong camp.*

January 1981

Wuyipeng [the Wolong research base] lies at 8,200 feet. Pandas roam to 10,500 feet and higher, as far as bamboo persists. Though gripped by winter cold, the forest is strangely verdant. There are spruce and hemlock and beneath them rhododendrons and whole slopes of bamboo, all in green leaf, as if summer has been momentarily suspended. . . .

Crossing a snow-covered swale are the tracks of a panda, days old. Yet they transform the forest, adding an aura of the remote, exotic, and mysterious. Hu Jinchu [coleader of the study] points to where the panda has bitten off a bamboo stem, eaten a portion, and discarded the top. It is a young stem, last year's shoot. Nearby I find a dropping, spindle-shaped and composed entirely of stem. I wonder how a panda can sustain itself on such coarse forage. The stems have barely been chewed and seem to have passed through the gut undigested. . . .

But there are limits to the amount of excitement that contemplation of a dropping can provide. Noting that the panda has angled downhill, we too descend, pushing our way through the bamboo in the general direction of Wuyipeng.

February 1981

Much of February was devoted to collecting the small and mundane facts which will ultimately, one hopes, reveal the habits and needs of the panda. For instance, my wife, Kay, who joined us early in the month, has the task of analyzing droppings to determine not only which species of bamboo the panda has eaten but also the proportion of stems to leaves. She dries the droppings in an oven that perches on the small woodstove in our tent. Wet samples awaiting processing and dry ones ready for sorting are by necessity scattered around the tent, on trunks, table, any available surface: the place at times resembles a stable.

A rare snowfall finds Hu Jinchu and me tracking pandas beneath a gloomy sky. The bamboo is bowed with snow, and as we press through it the stems shed their icy burdens down our necks. In some places the bamboo is so dense that we must crawl; in others only tenuous hand-holds on brittle shrubs keep us from tumbling down some steep pitch. At intervals a compacted area of snow littered with bamboo remnants reveals where a panda sat to feed. With fingers so numb from cold that they can barely hold a pencil, and shivering in our sodden clothes, we record the age of each stem eaten and measure the remnants. . . . To trace the route of a panda for a bit over a mile may take all day. Under such uncomfortable conditions there are no thoughts about the romance of fieldwork. . . .

Not all our work includes tedium and discomfort. There are moments of quiet pleasure too: A subadult panda has traveled down a snow slope and I follow its tracks. Wherever there is a small clearing, without bamboo or brush, the panda toboggans downhill on its chest and belly, no doubt delighted with its winter sport. Howard Quigley, who traced a different section of the animal's route, found a place where it had glissaded down, then walked back uphill to repeat its solitary game.

There are exciting happenings as well: A panda passed within one hundred feet of our tent before dawn, and its tracks in fresh snow reveal that it was traveling steadily and at an angle uphill. Some five hundred feet away were the tracks of a second and smaller animal moving in the same direction. All day we traced their routes, trying to discover where they had come from and where they were going. Late in the afternoon we not only found them but also observed that they had found each other.

A lone spruce rises tall and straight from a bamboo thicket. Near the tip of a bough, some fifty feet above ground, crouches a small panda, perhaps three years old. Below, among the lower limbs, sits a massive panda. Hu and I infer that the youngster has sought refuge in the tree after being chased by the adult, but being unable to determine the sex of the animals, we do not know the basis for the antipathy. Twice the young panda sends a long-drawn hoot plaintively across the silent and snowbound hills. We see the adult panda slide down the tree

My principal coworker, Hu Jinchu, holds a panda cub that was found alone in the forest. Local people presumed it had been abandoned by its mother and took it to a panda rescue center.

hind feet first and disappear, and we watch the youngster seek a secure seat before dusk and fog obscure our view.

As we turn toward Wuyipeng, we grin at each other with pleasure. Every project does have its romantic and exciting moments.

March 1981

. . . After many days of checking empty traps, the news that a panda has been caught electrifies the camp. Zhou Shu De comes to me leaping high and waving his arms and shouting that there is a panda in a trap at Juan Jin Gou, an hour's climb up and over the crest of a ridge. All equipment necessary for sedation, measuring, and radio-collaring is packed in rucksacks, ready for instant use, and we leave immediately to inspect the animal.

Zhen-Zhen, as we later name her, sits in the trap, hunched over, bleating plaintively to herself; occasionally she peers out between the bars with sad, uncomprehending eyes. We cluster a short distance from the trap trying to estimate her weight. An effective drug dose for sedation depends on the weight of an animal. Our consensus is about two hundred pounds.

Howard Quigley draws the proper dose into a syringe, and with the syringe attached to the end of a yard-long pole, he approaches the trap. Zhen-Zhen emits a screaming roar, startling in its intensity, and then another. Howard plunges the needle into her thigh. It is 9:09 A.M. He returns to us with a wry look, holding up the syringe: its needle has bent

Radio-collaring was an important tool when my Chinese and Western colleagues and I studied pandas in Wolong. Here I am taking notes while Howard Quigley and Hu Jinchu measure the sedated Zhen-Zhen. PHOTO BY KAY SCHALLER.

on Zhen-Zhen' s tough hide. He tries again. "OK, got her," he says, and we now wait for the drug to take effect. Within a few minutes her head droops but she remains awake; then, with a small additional dose, she reclines in deep sleep, and we pull her from the trap at 9:37. Her pulse is 68, her breathing steady.

Howard measures her and I record the numbers he calls out; Pan Wenshi searches for ectoparasites but finds none; Hu Jinchu checks her teeth to get an idea of her age. We fasten the one-and-a-half-pound radio collar around her neck, loose enough for comfort but tight enough to prevent it from being pulled off. We all assist in weighing her. And constantly I monitor her breathing. After a while her eyes focus and her eyelashes flutter; at 10:35 she barks suddenly and swats with a paw. It is obviously time to let her recover peacefully, and Howard and I pull her back into the trap. We open the trap door at 11:45. Though steady on her feet and fully alert, Zhen-Zhen does not seem to realize that she is now free. Finally, after half an hour, she peers out tentatively, then trots off through the bamboo at a fast pace, only the agitated stalks briefly revealing her route. . . .

April 1981

During April, ice vanished from the stream banks and snow retreated up the ravines. Flocks of blood pheasants broke up to nest; scarlet minivets, Gould's sunbirds, and other species returned from warmer climates. Lavender primroses carpeted slopes, and later in the month, the pink, white, purple, and yellow blossoms of rhododendrons filled the somber forests with color. Bamboo shoots pushed up through the dead leaves. Scattered groups of golden monkeys joined, forming one band with more than two hundred members. Wood mice in and around our tent began to reproduce, and the giant panda had his annual mating season. Spring had come to Wuyipeng. . . .

Radio-tracking told us that the old female Zhen-Zhen was unusually restless. Several hundred feet from her, on a gentle saddle densely covered with bamboo, a male had settled with his center of activity around a stand of tall fir. For at least two evenings he called, emitting the whines and barks that are the equivalent of a panda love song. To broadcast his presence more effectively, he climbed a fir and sent his calls across the valleys from up among the boughs.

A few days later Zhen-Zhen joined the male. Also attracted by the calls was a second male. The trio remained together for a frenzied several hours. The second and smaller male tried to approach Zhen-Zhen but was repeatedly chased away by the other male, who circled her protectively and copulated whenever she accepted him. Twice, when his attentions became too persistent, Zhen-Zhen climbed a tree to rest; he remained below, gently bleating. Standing nearby, hidden behind a fir, I was pleased to have a clear view of Zhen-Zhen. Since most of the activity was taking place in dense bamboo, I could monitor it mainly by the squeals, growls, moos, barks, bleats, and other discordant barnyard noises that seem to characterize panda squabbling and courting. The pandas remained together into the night, but by the following morning they had separated, each animal returning to its usual solitary existence. . . .

October 1981

The bamboo is dense and head-high as we push through it in the direction of Zhen-Zhen's radio signal, Hu in the lead. About thirty feet ahead and slightly downhill, by a fallen tree, the bamboo suddenly sways and Zhen-Zhen trots toward us, emitting screaming roars. Hu retreats somewhat hurriedly and I do not tarry either, clambering up a nearby sapling. The angry panda veers and passes beneath me, halts, listens, and everything being silent, starts to follow Hu's trail. Then she changes her mind and merely waits motionless in the bamboo. From my vantage point, I can see a massive fir with a hollow base, a perfect den site; nothing moves within the dark shadows. After a few minutes, I hear the squawks of an infant panda there. As quietly as possible, I descend from my perch and retreat, happy to learn not only that Zhen-Zhen has a baby after all, but also that she is guarding it well.

November 1981

In late October, Zhen-Zhen abandoned her den, even though her infant was still too weak to stand, much less walk, and moved farther afield. Since she now seems to lack a fixed abode, she probably carries her off-spring with her while foraging. In early November, when radio location indicated that Zhen-Zhen was on the other side of a ridge from her former den, I examined the site. The floor of the tree cavity measures 36 x 38 inches and consists of a crude nest-cup composed of fragments of rotten wood, clawed from the inside wall of the trunk, and several surprisingly stout saplings and branches, bitten off and carried to the den from as far as thirty feet away. Although Zhen-Zhen had made a rudimentary effort at constructing a nest, it lacked any obvious comfort.

December 1981

It is December 22. The temperature stands at –9°C, and frost on the birch boughs glitters in the slanting morning sun as Kay and I climb the slope behind camp to fetch a Christmas tree. We have already selected a tree, or rather Zhen-Zhen has chosen it for us. For mysterious reasons

Our home in the forests of Wolong while we studied pandas was a tent with a bed and a woodstove; Kay gathers firewood.

she bit the top off a young fir early last fall, dragged it into her den, and leaned it against the wall, its branches spreading over her infant in the nest. We felt that Zhen-Zhen's tree would give Christmas a special meaning to everyone at Wuyipeng.

We are less than halfway up toward the abandoned den when repeated calls from far below penetrate the stillness. Insistently the calls continue from the direction of Bai Ai, or White Rock, a cliff near which we have a panda trap. Faintly we can distinguish the words *daxiong mao*, panda. A panda has been caught.

We hurry back to camp, pick up equipment, and with our coworkers approach the trap in which Zang Xianti found a large male during his morning round of checking traps. The animal sits hunched over, silent, so drawn into himself that he even ignores the needle which injects the sedating drug into his shoulder. He is a massive, middle-aged male, with blunted yellow-stained canines. I fasten the radio collar around his neck and we measure him. . . . Shortly after his release, the male travels up toward a high ridge, where I establish radio contact with him later that afternoon. The slowly paced signal indicates an inactive animal, and it remains so at dusk. Is the male asleep? Or has he somehow pulled off the collar, negating three weeks of trapping effort? That night, during the long hours before dawn when dark thoughts invade the mind, I lie in my sleeping bag and relive the collaring, mentally slipping my fingers between the panda's neck and the collar to see that it is not too tight yet not so loose that the animal can slip it over his ears. Surely the collar must still be on the panda. Yet doubts remain with me in the morning as Kay and I once again follow the snow trail toward Zhen-Zhen's den.

Kay lifts the tree gently from the hollow. It is a little over a yard long. Some of its needles have fallen, there are tooth marks on the stem, and Zhen-Zhen has failed to select for symmetry. But we are delighted with our choice. While Kay takes the tree back to camp, I climb higher and tune the radio receiver to 197, the male's frequency. The signal is rapid, the animal active. All is well.

194

The next day, December 24, after monitoring the pandas and checking traps, Kay and I trim the tree in our tent with simple ornaments we have brought to remind us of home and other Christmases in distant places. There are paper Santa Clauses made by our children when small, a wooden chickadee which perched on a Christmas bough in the home of the mountain gorilla over two decades ago, and cutouts of animals, made from the lids of milk tins, to decorate a tree in the jungles of central India. Now we add miniature golden monkeys and pandas, given us by Chinese friends. In the evening we celebrate quietly by ourselves, exchanging small presents, eating fruitcake sent by Hong Kong friends, listening to Beethoven and Mendelssohn.

On Christmas Day, the leaders of Wolong provide us with a banquet at Wuyipeng. We move Zhen-Zhen's tree into the communal shed and place beneath it small presents, such as pens and flashlights, for our coworkers and for visitors who have come to celebrate with us.... Two cooks have been preparing dishes all day, and they now bring course after course.... During the meal I hand out gifts; we in turn receive a panda painting and a panda calendar. And in typical Chinese fashion, our banquet is interrupted by frequent speeches.

Hu Jinchu rises and announces: "We have decided on a name for the male panda we caught three days ago. His name is Wei-Wei." Wei-Wei means "grand." Hu's speech is followed by a toast to the male and ends with the word *gambe*, meaning cheers, bottoms-up, as we empty our glasses. Bi Fengzho, a leader in the Chengdu Forest Bureau, toasts our project and notes: "The best Christmas present is that another panda has been caught."

February 1982

No one has seen old Zhen-Zhen since October; only the radio signal reveals her continued presence in the usual area. Since tracking her in snow has never revealed any footprints of a youngster, we presume that her infant died. . . .

May 1982

Zhen-Zhen sits hunched, muzzle tucked into her folded arms, the white of her pelage glowing softly in the twilight of the bamboo. Silently I approach to within eighty feet of the dozing animal and there wait, partly screened by rhododendron. She raises her massive head and with an innocent, almost blank gaze looks at me. She snorts, then bleats softly in agitation, but does not flee; instead, she leans forward again, her back to me, to continue her rest. Each creature has its own window on reality, and I wonder what the world looks like to a panda. There is a startling self-assurance, a striking kind of freedom, in the way Zhen-Zhen ignores me today. At intervals she changes her position, sleeping on side or belly, and occasionally she sits up to scratch or paw flies off her face. After two and a half hours, with the onset of a heavy rain, she raises her arms above her head, stretches, yawns, and vigorously begins to munch bamboo shoots, consuming thirteen shoots in seventeen minutes, before dissolving into the shadows.

Zhen-Zhen permitted this rare glimpse into her life only a few days before I left for home . . . and I am grateful to her for this parting gift. . . .

I left Zhen-Zhen in her bower of bamboo, a gentle and brave and lonely survivor who with others of her kind must fade away unless humankind devotes itself to her future. But the very fact that this project exists is to her an implied promise of the Peaceable Kingdom.

[1987]

A Golden Horde

Mongolian Gazelle

My initial research on Mongolian gazelles so impressed me with the importance of maintaining their great herds that the Wildlife Conservation Society
began a long-term conservation program. Saiga antelope in Kazakhstan and
chiru, or Tibetan antelope, on the Tibetan Plateau had both declined drastically
during the 1990s, mainly due to illegal hunting. The Mongolian gazelles now
represented the last great migration in Asia. The threats to them are real, with
roads, oil drilling, and other development encroaching on the steppes, and with
thousands being shot for food each year. Weather is unkind to the gazelles as
well: many died in 1998 when heavy rains caused foot rot, and two years later
blizzards and extreme cold killed many more through hypothermia.

Kirk Olson, a graduate student at the University of Massachusetts, and
several Mongolian coworkers took on the task of studying the species. They
found that the gazelles have no consistent migratory routes but range widely
across the steppe in search of good pasture. No reserve can contain them; they
need the whole landscape. Veterinarians now monitor diseases, such as foot-
and-mouth, in both gazelles and livestock. Kirk has also counted gazelles—there
are at least one million—to provide a basis for management, and he has
conducted household interviews with the nomadic herders to learn about their
attitudes, how many gazelles they kill (an average of eight per household
yearly), and other information. Mongolia considers the gazelles an economic
resource that can be harvested sustainably. By collecting critical information
about the gazelles, the rangelands, and the people, we hope to ensure that the

*herds will remain as both a valuable resource and one of the world's great
wildlife spectacles.*

⚘

The Mongolian gazelles poured over the ridge and hurried northward
along the hill. First there were hundreds, then thousands, a tawny flood
of animals on migration. The date was July 19, 1993, less than a month
since the females had given birth. While the air vibrated to the code of
yips and bleats by which mother and offspring keep contact in the moving throng, Jeffrey Griffin, a conservationist working with the United
Nations Development Program (UNDP), and I set up our tents. Still the
gazelles came, their coats golden in the evening sun. How many had
passed so far? At least 25,000, we guessed. The Mongolian steppes are
usually associated with the pounding hooves of Genghis Khan's
mounted warriors. Now, as I lay in my tent, the steppes still reverber-
ated with sounds, but they were benign, the patter of tiny hooves and
birdlike gazelle cries.

We were witness to one of the world's great wildlife spectacles—
one that few people have ever seen. Wildebeest in the Serengeti, caribou
in the Arctic, Tibetan antelope (chiru) in China, saiga in Kazakhstan—
these are or were the notable ungulate (hoofed mammals) migrations.
In the steppes of eastern Mongolia, within an area of 100,000 square
miles, well over a million—perhaps as many as two million—gazelles,
Procapra gutturosa, persist, the largest concentration of any large mammal in Asia. I had first marveled at these herds in 1989; I was in
Mongolia again, this time on behalf of the UNDP to evaluate the conservation measures necessary to protect and manage the steppes and the
gazelles, symbols of this boundless space.

The steppes of eastern Mongolia comprise the biggest expanse of
unspoiled grassland in the world. No longer are there living reminders
of America's pristine prairies, but on Mongolia's steppe one can still
relive the past. Here, an endless sea of knee-high feather grass ripples in

198

More than a million Mongolian gazelles still roam the eastern steppes of Mongolia in huge herds, sometimes of 25,000 or more—the last such spectacle in Asia. Gazelle herds are always on the move, migrating in search of forage.

the wind, without fence or building to interrupt the immense sweep of land. Once America had bison. Mongolia still has gazelles, and nomadic herders with horses, cattle, and sheep are sparse because there is little surface water.

The future of these gazelles is not secure, however. Formerly found from Kazakhstan to northern China, populations now survive only in

Fresh water is scarce on the steppes, and in times of drought the gazelles crowd into a seepage.

Mongolia and in a narrow strip along China's border with Mongolia, where most are seasonal visitors, as well as a few in Russia. In the past four decades in China, at least 2.5 million gazelles were slaughtered for their meat.

In Mongolia, the species' range has shrunk by more than 50 percent since the 1950s. A railroad—fenced on both sides and running between Ulaanbaatar, Mongolia's capital, and Beijing—cuts across a main gazelle migration route, becoming a death trap for any animal trying to surmount the barbed wires. In addition, gazelles migrating between Mongolia and China face a fusillade from border guards. And almost every herdsman supplements his larder with gazelle meat. Illegal commercial hunts, sometimes with automatic weapons, provide meat to entire towns. One estimate places the illegal kill at over 100,000 gazelles a year. According to a 1995 law, the fine for each animal poached is the equivalent of $30 to $40, but there is little enforcement.

Official commercial hunting began in 1932, and annual kills often numbered more than 50,000 gazelles, with the meat exported principally to eastern Europe. In the past few years, this meat has been used within Mongolia—30,000 gazelles were slaughtered in 1997—or exported to China. The species could easily be managed and exploited sustainably, but the level of poaching undermines any attempt to do so.

Plans to develop the steppes also are cause for concern. Oil extraction has already begun, and there is talk of building a railroad eastward into China. Growing numbers of people, roads, fences, and livestock, as well as poaching, threaten the gazelles and their traditional migration routes.

No land mammal migrates more relentlessly: gazelle herds never settle in any one place. No reserve can contain them. A blunt Mongolian proverb states: "Whoever tells you where to find the gazelles at any given time is a liar." Unless the steppes are maintained as an intact ecosystem, only the memory of gazelle migrations will remain as part of the country's heritage, just as Genghis Khan is now an iconic memory of the distant past.

Despite the problems, Jeff and I were enchanted by the spacious freedom of the steppes, by the Mongolian larks and demoiselle cranes, pikas and marmots, silver sage and yellow-flowered *Caragana* shrubs. Something needed to be done to help the animals and their habitat endure. To our astonishment we learned that little was known about the gazelles—and this remains true today. Their migration routes are but vaguely understood. Neither the grasslands nor the ecological needs of the gazelles have been studied. How long do they live? What are the causes of death? How much relentless hunting can the species tolerate and still sustain itself?

I was told that the females gather briefly at traditional calving grounds in late June. To observe this critical period in the annual cycle, Badamjavin Lhagvasuren, of the Mongolian Academy of Sciences, and I spent a month this past summer in the steppes south of Choibalsan, the largest town in eastern Mongolia. Lhagva, as Mongolia's gazelle expert is called, has been involved with the species since 1981.

We set up camp on a plain bordered by rolling hills. Here the females come to give birth, according to a herdsman who had erected his yurt, or *ger* as it is known in Mongolia, by the only well in the region. Nearby, thousands of gazelles surge restlessly back and forth in small herds and aggregations of hundreds, sometimes running full tilt for no apparent reason. On occasion, tens of thousands gather in the evening, only to disperse by morning. Even the heavily pregnant females do not settle down, though the steppe is green with nutritious grasses, their main food that season. This constant shifting apparently segregates the sexes to some extent. Adult males tend to hang around the calving ground's periphery, often in bachelor clubs, and with them are many year-old males who have recently left their mothers.

On June 22, we see a female lying in feather grass. Soon a wet head on a shaky neck rises up, the first young of the season. Still, herds move on. Females that have given birth stay behind with offspring, which spend the first few days of life curled up, hidden in the vegetation. Newborns, however, are remarkably precocial, unlike other gazelle species in which offspring may remain secluded for two weeks or more. We watch one female give birth, then lick her young. At the age of twenty-two minutes, it tries to stand up but tumbles over. Finally, at fifty-seven minutes, after many stumbling attempts, it stands up and walks. Twenty-five minutes later it suckles. And at the age of one and a half hours, the newborn male, weighing nine pounds, is led away by its mother.

We know his sex and weight because we have caught and released him and eighty others. The sex ratio is equal, and weights vary from seven-pound listless young, who will most likely die, to a robust thirteen pounds. To find young, we walk across the steppe until we spot a motionless mound, the color of the sandy soil. While I make myself conspicuous, drawing the newborn's attention, Lhagva crawls up from behind and pounces, hoping the animal does not bolt. Attempts to catch young less than a day old are often successful, whereas older ones are usually too alert and flee.

202

The birth season gathers momentum. Between June 28 and July 4, an explosion of newborns litters plain and hill where the females have gathered. Two-thirds of all young are born in that week. Apparently excited by the birthing, the few males that remain in the area court females as they would in the December rut. They raise their muzzles and give hollow grunts, their goiterlike larynx bobbing up and down. The unusually large larynx apparently acts as an echo chamber. Males also try to mount females giving birth and vigorously chase them,

I crawl up close to a newborn gazelle to catch and weigh it. My Mongolian colleague, Badamjavin Lhagvasuren, and I did this many times during our work in the calving grounds; only day-old calves could be captured easily this way.

though both head and forelegs of the newborn may have already emerged. One male gores a female deep into her chest; she dies in childbirth. Her offspring dies also.

Otherwise the calving season progresses placidly. The sun shines warmly, there are no bothersome insects, and predators are few—some roaming dogs, an occasional red fox.

The attitude of Mongolians toward wolves is similar to that of most Americans earlier this century: kill every last one, if possible. To my regret, we do not meet any wolves. But there are steppe eagles, and the huge cinereous vultures are also known to kill newborn gazelles. We find the remains of one young that had been killed by a raptor and two that had been attacked and escaped, only to die from puncture wounds made by a bird's talons.

Luckily no poachers are in our area. A few days later, near Choibalsan, we find the butchered remains of three gazelles, including two females. We also spot a jeep loaded with gazelle carcasses. When we surprise two horsemen bearing two males they had shot, one explains, "We want meat for Naadam," referring to the upcoming national holiday.

Even at the height of calving, the females remain restless, as if begrudging these few days when newborns restrain their travels. Bands of mothers often wander off in the morning, leaving their offspring untended, waiting, until their return late in the day. By the age of one week, youngsters accompany their mothers on these seemingly random treks.

Gazelle herds are skittish. The animals know that people and cars mean death, and they may flee in panic. We are careful not to approach too closely, because if a young becomes separated from its mother while still dependent on her for milk it will die of starvation. No other female will foster it.

All but a few females have given birth by July 7. Then, as if by some mysterious, prearranged signal, the gazelles start to congregate. During calving they have been spread over at least four hundred square miles. Now herds hurry from the north and south and east to a great gathering. Their week or so of semisedentary life is over; the imperative of their race to move, move toward the far horizon, has reasserted itself.

On our last evening, Lhagva and I stand on a hill. Below us, gazelles crowd the slope and spread into the plain. The sun's soft rays touch them, transforming the massed animals into a flow of golden honey. To our right, thousands of gazelles glint, tiny points of light moving west into shadowed hills. We strive to protect such memories. As the magic moment passes into dusk, we share the hope that the great herds will always roam the steppes with unrestricted freedom.

[1998]

THE HIMALAYA AND
THE TIBETAN PLATEAU

This center of heaven.
This core of the Earth,
This heart of the world
Fenced round with snow.
The heartland of all rivers,
Where the mountains are high and
The land is pure.

—Anonymous sixth-century Tibetan poet

Nature and wild animals are complementary. People who live among wildlife without harming it are in harmony with the environment. Some of that harmony remains in Tibet, and because we had this in the past, we have some genuine hope for the future. If we make an attempt, we can have all this again.

—Tenzin Gyatso, H. H. the Dalai Lama

Ghost of the Hindu Kush

Snow Leopard

Whenever I walk through the Bronx Zoo, I like to halt in front of the snow leopards. Their luxuriant smoke-gray coats sprinkled with black rosettes convey an image of snowy wastes, and their pale, frosty eyes remind me of immense solitudes. For a moment the city vanishes and I am back in the Hindu Kush, the home of these magnificent cats.

I met the snow leopard described in this chapter more than three decades ago, when the part of Pakistan that holds the remote Hindu Kush Mountains was still known as West Pakistan. Yet this one encounter left me with an insistent memory and a desire to encounter the cat again. Beyond the exhilaration of exploring mountains, just being in a place with snow leopards puts everything into a new dimension: I imagined what was invisible to the eye. I did find spoor in China and Tajikistan, and also glimpsed a cat in Nepal, but only in Mongolia—where snow leopards may reside in desert mountains at elevations of only 3,000 feet—was I able to study them briefly by attaching radio collars to two animals.

Fortunately, others are devoting their lives to gathering knowledge about this endangered mountain spirit, of which perhaps four thousand to seven thousand live scattered in a dozen Central Asian countries. Rodney Jackson of the Snow Leopard Conservancy did the first thorough study in Nepal during the early 1980s, and Thomas McCarthy of the International Snow Leopard Trust worked in Mongolia during the 1990s. They and others continue the effort to protect the cat.

It is a difficult task. A snow leopard may travel over 10 to 150 square miles of rugged terrain, the size of its range depending on the abundance of such prey as bharal, ibex, and marmots. Density is generally low, often no more than one cat per 40 square miles. When local people decimate its natural prey, the cat may turn to livestock—and in turn get killed. Various programs have attempted to reduce such retaliatory killing by offering communities economic incentives in exchange for protecting all wildlife; these include establishing small handicraft industries, training herders in better livestock protection, paying direct compensation, turning over most funds derived from official trophy hunts, and setting up an insurance scheme by which a cash payment is made for each head of livestock lost.

Such efforts are valuable but have only a local impact. The snow leopard's best chance of survival at present is to glide unseen, like a wisp of cloud, through its vast mountain realm.

December cold gripped the valley as soon as the feeble sun disappeared behind the ridge. The slopes and peaks above an altitude of 11,000 feet were snow-covered, and a bank of clouds along the distant summits suggested that soon so would be the valleys. I hurried down the trail along the edge of a boulder-strewn stream until the valley widened. There I stopped and with my binoculars scanned the steep slope ahead, moving upward past the scree and outcrops, past scattered oak trees and stands of pine, to a cliff over a thousand feet above me. A female snow leopard lay on the crest of a spur, her chin resting on a forepaw, her pelage blending into the rocks so well that she seemed almost a part of them. Several jungle crows sat in a nearby tree, and a Himalayan griffon vulture wheeled overhead, intent, I knew, on the carcass of a domestic goat that the leopard was guarding.

I angled up the slope toward her, moving slowly and halting at intervals, trying to seem oblivious to her presence. She flattened into the rocks and watched my approach. Once she sat up, her creamy white

In 1973 I had several sightings of this female snow leopard in the Hindu Kush
Mountains of the Chitral area, northern Pakistan. She lies near a jumble of boulders
in which her single cub is hidden.

chest a bright spot among the somber cliffs, then snaked backward off
her vantage point to become a fleeting shadow that molded itself to the
contours of the boulders. She retreated uphill, crossing open terrain
only when a tree or outcrop shielded her from my view. From another
rock she peered at me, only the top of her head visible, but a few minutes later she stalked back to her original perch and casually reclined
there. I was grateful for her curiosity and boldness, for she was so adept
at hiding that I would not have seen much of her without her consent. I
halted 150 feet away, and in the fading light unrolled my sleeping bag
along a ledge in full view of her. Lying in the warmth of my bag, I could
observe her feeding at the kill until darkness engulfed us. And then there
was only the wind moaning among the boulders, and the occasional
grating of tooth on bone as the leopard continued her meal.

That night it snowed, heavy moist flakes that soaked through my
bedding. I huddled on the ledge, sleeping intermittently, until the rocks

Markhor goats, with their distinctive spiraling horns, are a main prey of snow leopard in the Chitral area. This young male looks across a valley to the towering Hindu Kush.

once again emerged from the darkness. Over four inches of snow had fallen. As I rolled up my sodden belongings, I envied the snow leopard, which sat protected and dry in the shelter of an overhang. I descended the slope through clouds and falling snow, heading toward the mud-walled hut that was my base camp in the valley. Though I was tired and chilled, the mere thought of having spent the night near a snow leopard filled me with elation.

With the support of the New York Zoological Society and the National Geographic Society, Zahid Beg Mirza of the Punjab University and I had come to Chitral in Pakistan to make a monthlong wildlife survey in the Chitral Gol reserve. This reserve, comprising about thirty square miles of rugged mountains with peaks rising to an altitude of 17,500 feet, has for many years belonged to the royal family of Chitral. His Highness Saif-ul-Mulk hopes to convert the area from a hunting reserve into a private sanctuary where visitors might observe the wildlife. Of particular interest to us were the Kashmir markhor goats, one of seven subspecies of *Capra falconeri.*

The markhor spend May to October at timberline and above, but they winter in the valleys where there is less snow and more food. In the Chitral Gol, evergreen oak trees provide the markhor with their main winter forage. It was startling to see these goats clamber with amazing agility among the branches of an oak tree, as high as twenty feet above ground, as they searched for tender twigs and leaves. Most of the herds we saw were small, ranging from two to eighteen individuals, and usually consisted of several females, many of them accompanied by one or two kids, a yearling or two, and often some young males. Each herd tended to confine its movements to a particular locality.

On the other hand, the adult males, easily recognizable by their long, spiraling horns and flowing white neck ruff, roamed widely, either alone or in small groups. In late November and early December, some adult males joined the females in the herds, the first sign of the rut which was to reach its peak in late December. Only one large adult male accompanied a herd during the rut, a good indication that at that time relations between rivals were strained. Our census showed that about 100 to 125 markhor wintered in the reserve. The population was healthy and breeding was good. An average of 1.3 kids accompanied each adult female, and 16.5 percent of the population consisted of yearlings. If poaching could be fully controlled and the range less heavily used by domestic stock, the Chitral Gol might some day become the most important refuge for this increasingly rare goat.

One day, shortly after our arrival, we found old snow leopard tracks crossing a snowdrift at 11,000 feet, and I became determined to meet one of these cats. Snow leopards live in the mountains of Central Asia, usually occurring above an altitude of 5,000 feet, although in some areas, such as the Dzhungarian Ala-Tau of the [former] USSR, they are found as low as 3,000 feet. Their range extends from the Hindu Kush in Afghanistan eastward along the Himalayas and across Tibet to Sichuan Province in China, and northeastward along the Pamir, Tien Shan, and

Altai ranges to the Sayan mountains that straddle the border between Mongolia and Russia near Lake Baykal.

Because of its remote habitat, coupled with its shy nature and rarity, the snow leopard remains the least known of the great cats. Most published accounts say little more than that they migrate seasonally up and down the mountains with the herds of wild sheep and goats that constitute their principal prey. Only occasionally do such accounts contain an interesting bit of information. In the Khirgiz Ala-Tau, for instance, snow leopards are said to rest in nests built by black vultures in low juniper trees, and a Russian biologist watched two snow leopards play, rearing up on their hind legs and exchanging blows before "arching their backs at one another" and parting. Hari Dang, an Indian mountaineer, has seen snow leopards repeatedly, and his article "The Snow Leopard and Its Prey," published in the October 1967 issue of the journal *Cheetal*, represents the best attempt so far to gather information about this elusive cat.

For a week I searched for snow leopards, following tracks until they disappeared among the crags. A snow leopard in a zoo may mark its cage by rubbing its face sinuously against a log, scraping the floor alternately with its hind paws, and then turning, its tail raised and quivering, and squirting a mixture of scent and urine. At other times, it may scrape and then defecate at the site. Now, in the wild, I found similar signs. Occasionally a pungent odor on a tree trunk or rock told me where a snow leopard had left its "calling card," and scrapes, with or without feces, also advertised its presence. The feces revealed what the animals had eaten. I examined sixteen droppings, and of these, five contained markhor hair, eight the remains of domestic sheep and goats, two solely a large-leafed herb, and one just earth.

Judging by tracks, a female with a cub and a small lone animal, probably a subadult, frequented the Chitral Gol during our visit, but other snow leopards no doubt also roamed through the area at times. The tracks showed that snow leopards, like most cats, were essentially solitary except, of course, when a female had cubs. Hari Dang saw snow leopards sixteen times, of which twelve sightings were of animals alone and the rest of pairs. But whether the pairs consisted of a male and a female, a large cub with its mother, or members of the same sex was not specified. Nothing is known about the social system of snow leopards, and I wonder if adults are truly unsociable, like the African leopard, or if they may meet, tarry a while together, and perhaps share a kill before parting again, as is the case among tigers.

I soon realized that my chances of meeting a snow leopard were slim. The cats were rare, and they traveled far each day in search of food. The large herds of domestic sheep and goats that forage on the alpine meadows in summer had been taken to the villages. Marmots were hibernating. All that remained were scattered herds of markhor and various small animals, such as black-naped hare and chukar partridge, which could provide a snack at most for a predator that may weigh as much as one hundred pounds and reach a length of 6.5 feet.

The lack of food in winter may force snow leopards into the cultivated valleys, where they lurk around villages with the hope of capturing an unwary dog or other domestic animal. Often they are rewarded with a bullet instead. The demand for spotted furs by the fashion industry has also provided an incentive for killing the cats. Although both India and Pakistan prohibit the commercial export of snow leopard, any number of skins can be bought in local markets for about $150 apiece and smuggled without trouble out of these countries in personal luggage. The International Fur Trade Federation has agreed to impose a total ban on trade in snow leopard skins among its members, a step that will hopefully reduce the demand for this fur.

Having obtained some idea of the favored routes of the snow leopards in the Chitral Gol, I staked out a domestic goat as bait at five different locations. Daily for two weeks I checked each goat, feeding and watering it when necessary, yet the cats eluded me. One night a snow leopard passed within 150 feet of a goat, apparently without seeing it, for the tracks continued without deviation or break in stride.

I had almost given up hope of a meeting when early one morning a sanctuary guard hurried toward me, pointing with his stick at the sky and grinning broadly. Circling high over a ridge near one of the goats were several vultures. A kill had been made. And then through my scope I saw the snow leopard at rest on a promontory. Beside her was a tiny cub, a black-and-white puff of fur about four months old. In captivity the usual litter consists of two cubs, but litters vary from one to four young. Later I was told by the sanctuary staff that this female had been seen with two cubs the previous month. According to the literature, cubs are usually born in April and May. Assuming a gestation period of 98 to 103 days, as determined in zoos, this cub had been conceived at that time and been born in August.

Soon afterward the cub retreated into a cleft among the rocks and remained out of sight all day, while its mother continued to guard the kill. Once a bold crow landed near the carcass and the female rushed at the bird, her movements remarkably smooth in spite of her stocky, powerful build. Afterward she reclined again, dozing or gazing over her domain. At dusk the cub rejoined its mother, greeting her in typical cat fashion by rubbing its cheek against hers. They then fed. On subsequent days they followed the same routine, with the result that I seldom was able to observe the cub.

Daily for a week I watched the snow leopards, sometimes concealed on the opposite side of the valley, at other times near them. I moved a little closer each day until the female permitted me to approach to within 120 feet. Since she spent hour after hour at rest and the cub remained hidden, my behavioral observations were rather limited in scope.

At times I was able to watch a herd of markhor on a distant slope. The rut was now reaching its peak. If there was a female in heat, a large male might follow her closely, holding himself very erect until suddenly he lowered his neck and stretched his muzzle forward while his tongue flicked in and out of his mouth. With a jerk he twisted his head sideways, at the same time kicking a foreleg into the air. To this display the female markhor would often respond by walking hurriedly away. The

I observed this snow leopard for a week but saw her cub only fleetingly during that time.

male followed, which in turn caused her to move faster, until both rushed along the slope and through the trees.

At other times there were birds to observe. Two bearded vultures might be tumbling over and over in a display of aerial exuberance, their hawklike screams the only sounds among these snow-flecked crags, or I might tally the bird species that passed by me—alpine chough, nutcracker, black-throated jay, pied woodpecker, and others.

After the snow leopards had eaten one goat, I gave them another and then a third. The female killed the last one late in the afternoon, as I watched. She advanced slowly down the slope, body pressed to the ground, carefully placing each paw until she reached a boulder above the goat. There she hesitated briefly, then leaped to the ground. Whirling around, the startled goat faced her with lowered horns. Surprised, she reared back and swiped once ineffectually with a paw. When the goat turned to flee, she lunged in and with a snap clamped her teeth on its throat. At the same time she grabbed the goat's

217

shoulders with her massive paws. Slowly it sank to its knees, and when she tapped it lightly with a paw, it toppled on its side. Crouching or sitting, she held its throat until, after eight minutes, all movement ceased. Judging by tooth marks on the throat, she had also killed the two previous goats by strangulation.

Hari Dang once watched a snow leopard attack a Himalayan tahr, a type of wild goat: "We were lying behind a boulder watching the thar [sic] climbing leisurely up the scree and the rock overhangs towards the north ridge of Raj Ramba peak, when a flash of white and grey fur dived into the spread out herd, and rolled down some hundred feet, all the time hanging on to a young thar ewe." At that point the snow leopard was disturbed by the observer and fled. Dang noted further that, "of seventeen natural kills seen, eleven were deduced on the basis of the evidence of the tracks to have been made in daytime, generally the early morning and late afternoon." In contrast to my observations, he found that, of "thirty-four natural and domestic kills . . . most were neatly killed, either with the neck or the spine broken."

One night the snow leopards departed. I traced their tracks past some outcrops and through a stand of pine, before deciding to leave the animals in peace. My meeting with them had been brief, too brief to teach me much of consequence, but on seeing the line of tracks continue upward, I hoped that some day I would return and learn more about the life of these phantoms of the snow.

No one knows how many snow leopards inhabit the mountains of Central Asia, but the animal is thought to be rare enough to warrant inclusion in the Red Data Book of the world's threatened species. Though the habitat of the snow leopard seems inaccessible, pastoralists and hunters penetrate the remotest valleys and plateaus, shooting the cats and depriving them of their natural prey. Only large and strictly protected reserves may ultimately help the snow leopard to survive in the wild. Several reserves beside the Chitral Gol contain a few of the cats, among them, for example, the Nanda Devi and Dachigam Sanctuaries in India and the Aksu-Dzhabagly Sanctuary in Kazakhstan, but in South Asia they receive at best only the most cursory protection. Zoos are assuming increasing importance as repositories of breeding stock of threatened species. When in 1903 the Bronx Zoo received its first snow leopards, only two others were on exhibition elsewhere, in London and Berlin. By 1970, a total of ninety-six snow leopards resided in forty-two zoos, according to the *International Zoo Yearbook*. But of these only twenty were bred in captivity, a dismal record. Zoos still draw most of their animals from the wild, principally from the Tien Shan Mountains of Russia, because animals born in captivity seldom live to reproduce.

On seeing a snow leopard in a cage, I can forget the bars and remember when we met on a desolate slope in a world of swirling snow. May others, too, find such private visions until the end of time.

[1972]

Author's note: *I was, and still am, ambivalent about providing a snow leopard with live bait. I checked the goats twice a day to make certain that they remained fed and watered and were not distressed; they lacked only companionship. I could have offered dead baits, as is still done by hunters for lions and leopards, but that would have caused the death of goats needlessly. Most of the live goats were not discovered by a snow leopard in the few days they were tied out, and there was little chance that a cat would find a goat carcass before it was stripped by vultures. Furthermore, my heart is with the rare markhor, not the locust-like domestic goat. Each meal of a domestic goat eaten by a snow leopard saved the life of a markhor.*

I went on seeking snow leopards during various journeys in Nepal and Pakistan during the early 1970s, as related in my book Stones of Silence. *My rare contact with the cat nearly always took a form similar to that described in the following two accounts from Nepal. The first took place shortly after I arrived at Lapche monastery near the headwaters of the Bhote Kosi river; the second at Shey monastery, on the flanks of the sacred Crystal Mountain in Dolpo, where I studied bharal.*

With two hours of daylight left, I ambled toward Lapche village and almost immediately came across a snow leopard track, made since that night of the big snow. The cat had walked steadily toward the village and on into Tibet. Just before the village the tracks of a second snow leopard crossed those of the first—and it had dragged something uphill.

I followed the drag mark slowly, scanning the slope every few steps. By a large boulder were several depressions in the snow where the cat had been resting: it had seen my approach and fled. Fresh pugmarks showed where it had bounded away under the cover of a rise and vanished in a broken cliff. Nearby were the remains of a bharal, a male almost four years old. From spoor in the snow I reconstructed the course of events leading to his death. He had wandered alone around the village, then, angling into a shallow valley, had gone to a rivulet to

Our yak caravan traverses the Hindu Kush in search of snow leopards and other wildlife; I made several trips here in the early 1970s.

drink, his descent no doubt observed by the snow leopard. Its advance hidden by a boulder, the cat had stalked closer, and as the bharal stood by the water, it attacked, pulling its victim down at the point of impact. After disemboweling the animal and eating parts of the viscera and the rib cage, the snow leopard dragged the carcass some five hundred feet uphill to where I found it.

I checked the kill again at dawn. The last meat had been eaten during the night, and once again the cat had vanished unseen. It did not return. Five village men moved into the eastern valley, occupying a crude hut of stone walls roofed with old skins. They were there to cut grass on the snow-free slopes for livestock fodder. They also tried to accustom the yaks to being handled again after a feral existence all winter; they talked to them gently and fed them salt by hand until the shy beasts tolerated being touched. One of the men mentioned to Phu-Tsering that he had heard a snow leopard calling in the valley at dusk.

The next day I stopped alone by their hut to inquire about this. They sat cross-legged around a furiously boiling pot, and one motioned me to join them. They had slipped out of their sheepskin jackets, and matted hair hung to their bare shoulders. With long knives they fished in the foul-smelling pot for chunks of meat from a yak that had died a week ago. The plat du jour was decayed liver, of which I ate a polite portion. Although I have a strong stomach, it forcefully rejected this meal an hour later.

The men showed little interest in providing me with information about snow leopards. Vaguely and indifferently they indicated that it was somewhere, anywhere. Knowing that cats, like people, prefer to travel along easy routes, I seated myself above a well-worn yak trail and waited. Clouds descended the slopes, obscuring the lofty peaks as it grew dusky. In shadowy solitude I waited, huddled among dark boulders; it began to snow. Then out of the dark came a wailing miaow, a wild, longing sound from a creature doomed forever to wander these wastes searching for someone to share its fate. Minutes later, another miaow. And after that, silence.

᷽

Of the many mountain spirits at Shey, I seek to meet only one—the snow leopard. Peter [Matthiessen] and I had found an old dropping, but not until the morning of November 12, the day after Tukten and Gyaltsen returned, is there a fresh track in the dust of a trail. We peruse the slopes carefully, knowing the cat is there, perhaps watching us with clear, unblinking eyes, but only a golden eagle quarters the cliffs.

Again that night the snow leopard patrols the slopes in search of an unwary bharal. Near the hermitage trail is a shallow cave, and at its entrance I pile rocks into a low wall behind which I unroll my sleeping bag. Perhaps the snow leopard will pass my hiding place at dusk or dawn. I stretch a trip wire attached to a camera flash across the trail to record any nocturnal visitor. My afternoon vigil is futile, and finally the night cold sends me to bed. The cave's ceiling presses close, and in the dim light I can see in it scalloped shells, fragments of bryophytes, and calcareous tubes, probably the former retreats of marine worms. I lie among fossilized creatures of the ancient Tethys Sea, where, long before man, waves pounded and life pulsated in the abysmal depths. If I close my right eye, there is only rock; I lie buried beneath the sediments of the ocean floor, and perhaps my skull will become a *salegrami* stone. If I close the left eye, my gaze is liberated, penetrating the emptiness beyond the first evening stars.

The snow leopard crossed the slope just above my cave sometime during the night and joined the trail 150 feet beyond the trip wire. All that day and the next I look for its shadow among clefts and behind junipers. But spirits are made of dreams and their appearance cannot be willed. Before dawn on November 15, the snow leopard passes above the monastery, and that same night a lone wolf trots by our tents going the other way, leaving only tracks to reveal their furtive presence. After four days the snow leopard vanishes from Shey, without having caught a bharal. Scavenger birds would have told me of a kill.

[1980]

Grazing the Mountain's Edge

Bharal

Bharal, or blue sheep, have physical attributes of both sheep and goats, a fact that once elicited argument among taxonomists, who naturally like things tidy. Since an animal's behavior can supplement morphological criteria in determining where it fits in the taxonomic scheme of things, a study of this species was certainly warranted. Intrigued by the bharal, I trekked to the uplands of northern Nepal to settle at a monastery where, I had been told, blue sheep could be easily observed. The rather tedious listing and quantifying of different behaviors in this article may seem trivial, but it did help to clarify the situation. Later, DNA analysis confirmed that bharal are more closely related to goats than to sheep.

My long journey through the Himalaya toward the Tibet border did have a purpose beyond curiosity. Because the region had few people and a fair amount of wildlife, I wanted to evaluate it as a potential protected area. Subsequently a total of about 1,422 square miles was designated by Nepal as the Shey-Phoksundo National Park.

⚘

The valley widened, and then from a spur above the stream I saw Shey Gompa ahead. Huddled against a slope, the Buddhist monastery with its

223

To reach the bharal in Dolpo at the southern edge of the Tibetan plateau took a month of trekking, from the lowlands of Nepal across the Himalaya, with porters carrying our food and other supplies. The writer Peter Matthiessen joined me on this 1973 trip and later published his superb book The Snow Leopard.

attending cluster of sacred stupas and dwellings seemed lost in the folds of the Himalaya—an ancient world frozen in time. New York Zoological Society trustee Peter Matthiessen and I trudged on through the snow, the end of our journey finally in sight.

Over a month ago, on September 28, we had left the Nepalese town of Pokhara and walked westward along the flanks of the Dhaulagiri massif. Then, penetrating the Himalaya, we crossed icebound passes and traced turbulent rivers until we reached the village of Ringmo. To the north, in the heart of the Dolpo District adjoining Tibet, was Shey—a secret universe that few outsiders have visited. But to reach Shey we had to cross a 17,800-foot pass. Deterred by wintry blasts and deep snow, our fifteen porters abandoned us far from any village, leaving eight hundred pounds of food and equipment in a desolate mound on a patch of scree. However, our three Sherpa assistants remained with us, and together we hauled the supplies over the brittle crest of the pass.

During these weeks of trekking, as torrential rains and other obstacles hampered our advance, Shey began to represent more than just a place where I planned to study blue sheep. The monastery within its fortress of peaks became an existential quest of man testing himself against the indifference of the natural world, as well as a search for something intangible that seemed forever elusive. Yet now, as we finally approached Shey with our energies sapped by altitude and devouring cold, my only goal was a cup of hot tea.

When the naturalist Brian Hodgson first described the blue sheep in 1833, he gave it the scientific name *Ovis nayaur* on the assumption that it was a sheep rather than a goat. Indeed the animal resembles a sheep with its stout horns sweeping out and back, and with neither beard nor potent body odor. But in other traits—such as its broad flat tail, the striking black-and-white markings on its forelegs, and some skull characters—it is goatlike. Sheep have eye glands and they have pedal glands between their hooves, whereas goats lack eye glands and are equipped with pedal glands only on the forefeet, if at all. Blue sheep add to the confusion in that some individuals have rudimentary eye and pedal glands and others lack them. Thoroughly puzzled, Hodgson finally placed the animal into a separate genus, *Pseudois,* thirteen years after he had first named it. At present, the blue sheep is considered to be a goat with sheeplike affinities. Obviously the common name *blue sheep* is inappropriate and I will hereafter refer to the animal as bharal, as it is called in Hindi.

Behavioral information can sometimes supplement other data when solving taxonomic problems. Although travelers and hunters had encountered the bharal, no attempt was made to study its behavior before I became interested in the species. This is hardly surprising, for bharal live in one of the most remote regions on Earth, the Tibetan highlands and some bordering ranges. Their haunts are usually at high altitudes, from 13,000 feet upward to the limit of vegetation at 18,000 feet. Intrigued by this "sheep that isn't," I had chosen Shey as a study site because the local lama was rumored to have protected wildlife for many years. The first of Buddhist precepts, "I undertake the rule of training to refrain from injury to living things," is now practiced all too rarely in the Himalaya, making good research locations difficult to find.

By the time we arrived at Shey almost all of the villagers had moved with their livestock to lower altitudes for the winter. Seven of the eight houses in the village had been abandoned. With their high walls slashed by narrow window slits, they looked like fortresses, vaguely sinister, as if ready to defend themselves against the elements and other foes. In an annex of the monastery lived a woman with two small children. Her name was Tasi Chanjum, but she preferred to be called Namu, for among Tibetans it is impolite to address a person by his or her name. Namu was suspicious of strangers, but grudgingly she permitted us to occupy a hut consisting of a single sooty room just large enough to store our equipment, house the Sherpas, and permit us to crowd around the small earthen hearth. Peter and I set up our sleeping tents nearby.

The lama lived with a helper in a hermitage on the other side of the valley. As revealed by a Tibetan verse, a hermitage requires a certain type of location:

Gyab rii tag
Dun rii tso

The mountain rock behind;
The mountain lake in front.

Conforming to this tradition, the hermitage perched high on a cliff—an ocher-colored aerie with a view not of a lake but at least of a river.

To my delight, the 175 to 200 bharal in the area had little fear of man. They sometimes foraged around the deserted buildings and used the urine-splattered outdoor latrine of the lama as a saltlick. Every

I studied and photographed bharal, or blue sheep, in the Dolpo region of northwestern Nepal in 1973.

morning, well before the sun reached the slopes, I scanned the hills for bharal. At this early hour they foraged high up—at 15,000 feet or so—away from the biting cold of the valleys. Usually I could spot a herd or two from the door of the stone and mud hut we occupied. The animals were mere blue-gray dots on snow-free patches of ground. While some herds consisted of only three or four individuals, others numbered as many as sixty of all ages and both sexes. Over two hundred bharal have been seen together in other parts of their range. However, herd membership is flexible, with animals joining or parting at intervals.

Selecting one herd for detailed observation, I trudged upward, hurrying toward the sun that now crept down the slopes, bringing warmth to a bare sepia world. After a casual approach, I sat down about two hundred feet from the animals. They were seldom disturbed by my presence, although one occasionally emitted a chittering alarm call similar to that of an angry red squirrel.

For me, the first meeting with an animal that has been little studied is the most exciting part of a project. Even ordinary behavior becomes a basis for meaningful comparisons with other species, and a glimpse of something unique sends the mind on stimulating quests for evolutionary parallels. Having studied urial sheep, Persian wild goats, and markhor goats in Pakistan, I now looked for comparisons between them and the bharal.

The urial and other Eurasian sheep are delicately structured like antelope, adapted to plains and hills over which they can flee fast and far when disturbed. Seeing the chunky, powerful build of bharal, it was obvious that they were well designed for mountain climbing—resembling goats and American bighorn sheep in physique. Bharal like to forage on grassy slopes, being not at all partial to precipices, but the importance of their proximity to cliffs became startlingly clear one day.

Six bharal were grazing on a slope when suddenly two wolves—large, silvery-gray beasts—bounded downhill toward them, the speed of their attack hampered by the procumbent junipers over which they had to leap. Bunching up, the bharal raced to a cliff below. The wolves almost succeeded in overtaking a lagging female, but she angled sharply downhill, barely escaping onto a precipice. The foiled wolves returned up the slope, where they rejoined two others who had not participated in the chase. Six hours later the bharal still lingered near the safety of their cliff.

Among societies of hoofed animals, the most active time of year is the rut—a time when males strive vigorously for dominance, which in turn gives them priority to females in heat. I had timed our trip to coincide with the rut. Like most other species of high altitudes and northern latitudes, bharal mate in autumn and winter, and then give birth in May and June when the cold has passed and food is again plentiful for mother and young. However, nowhere in the literature had I been able to find out precisely when bharal mate. Now in early November the rut had not yet begun. Males generally ignored females, and some were still in bachelor herds. One such herd, numbering up to fourteen males, lived on the slope above the monastery, where I was able to observe it and gain valuable insights into the behavior of the animals.

Male sheep and goats are inveterate status-seekers. Unlike most antelope, they do not proclaim their rank by establishing and defending a territory, but instead carry their rank symbols with them in the form of special coat colors, large body size, and impressive horns. So it is with bharal. For example, only fully adult males have intensely black and swollen necks. However, their most important status symbol is horn length. Growing throughout the life of an animal, horns reflect the age and, by implication, the strength of the bearer. On meeting each other, two males can usually evaluate each other's fighting potential at a glance, and the smaller animal then defers to the larger. Even if the smaller refuses to accept his subordinate position with grace, a dominant male does not exhaust himself needlessly in asserting rank. Instead he conveys his status with such subtle behavior that at first I did not always recognize the true import of his quiet strivings. For example, one male might halt casually by a second one, standing broadside until the other just as casually averts his head in submission. Or two males might feed side by side until the subordinate animal moves forward. Should this happen, the other quickly noses ahead—it being the prerogative of the dominant to lead.

Bharal also use more blatant methods to express their dominance, as when one male mounts another. A dominant individual can do this with impunity, but he considers it an affront if a subordinate attempts it and he retaliates quickly. On occasion one male might also approach another with his neck lowered and muzzle stretched forward; then he may kick the other gently with a foreleg. Sheep often display dominance in this particular manner, whereas goats rarely do so. A bharal male may also extend his crimson penis threateningly while standing in a hunched position broadside to an opponent. Afterward he may insert his penis into his mouth. Sheep do not behave like this. But goats nuzzle their own penises and while doing so they may spray urine over their faces, the odor apparently enhancing their rank. While observing these and other displays, I realized that bharal behavior was in some ways intermediate between that of sheep and goats.

Two male bharal of similar size may have a dominance problem, with neither accepting the dictates of the other—a problem that can be settled only on the battlefield. On such occasions one male may rear bolt upright, standing balanced on his hind legs, and then, with head cocked sideways, lunge downward to crash his horns against those of his opponent, who is waiting to catch the blow. Or both may dash some twenty feet apart, rear up, and on their hind legs hop or run toward each other before bashing horns with a loud crack. Such fights were stunning (figuratively speaking) not only for their power but also for the almost ritualized violence that enabled the combatants to meet horns so precisely.

Goats fight much like bharal. However, urial sheep clash after running at each other on all fours, and American sheep rear up only partially and, with their bodies slanting forward, run to meet head-on. Both techniques differ from those of bharal.

A low-ranking bharal uses a curious gesture both to convey his submission and to express friendliness: he rubs his face all over the rump of the dominant animal, sometimes for a minute or more. Another even more subordinate male may join them and rub the second-largest male, the three then standing amicably in a row. In a society whose males are not always acquainted with each other and in which dominance is vigorously expressed, a friendly overture can be advantageous. Sheep rub faces, not rumps, and goats lack any gesture of this type, simply avoiding contact.

As if all this stressful status-seeking needed an innocuous outlet—a release of tension—bharal have also devised a method of communicating informally. Several males may interact seemingly at random; they mount, clash, and rub rumps without reference to dominance and without risk of retaliation. Sheep also have such free-for-alls, except that rams stand in a circle facing inward like players in a football huddle. Goats do not behave in this manner, one reason probably being that cliffs are not suitable for such huddling.

Some days I spent near female bharal and their young, watching them until the sun slipped behind a ridge and cold prowled the slopes again. Only two females out of five had young at heel, a surprisingly low number. And there were three times as many females as yearlings, indicating that the surviving crop of young from the previous year was small, too.

It is often assumed that losses of young are due mainly to predation. Indeed wolves passed through Shey six times during my stay there. One snow leopard hunted the slopes for four days (and caught nothing), and two others traveled through one night. Some 38 percent of the wolf droppings contained bharal remnants, and for snow leopards the figure was 50 percent. The remaining prey items consisted mainly of livestock and marmots—the latter available only from May to October, when they are not hibernating. Although some bharal fell prey, the evidence indicated that predators were not to blame for the poor crop of young.

Bharal males rear up to clash horns during the rut.

231

The vigor of a population depends on the condition of the range—on the food supply of the animals. When food is plentiful and nutritious, the well-fed females give birth to large, healthy young. When it is of low quality, the newborns are often weak and many soon die, their underfed mothers having little milk for them. Even a casual look showed that all was not well with the habitat at Shey. The slopes were eroded and crisscrossed by innumerable livestock trails. Much of the grass—the preferred food of bharal—was tucked beneath low-growing, thorny *Lonicera* shrubs, where it was difficult to reach. Here, as elsewhere in the Himalaya, domestic sheep, goats, and yaks graze nearly to the limit of vegetation in the summer, thereby competing with wildlife for forage. Domestic goats, in particular, are the "black sheep" among livestock in that they eat almost everything, even pulling plants out by the roots.

Observing bharal daily in the midst of this gigantic disorder of rock—the ocher canyon draining the Shey valley and the frieze of snow peaks guarding the Tibetan border—I found that research became more than just a quest for facts. Most men enjoy adventure: they want to explore the ranges beyond, and in the mountains a biologist can become a discoverer in a physical realm as well as an intellectual one. Mountains help one to grasp the reality of life, to integrate one's existence. Life ceases to be a fixed voyage. Instead the future possesses a vast unknown potential, becoming a journey, both outward and inward, as one struggles to survive and searches for a place in eternity.

I was impatiently waiting for the rut. It was late November, yet the adult males in the bachelor herd above the monastery were still interested only in dominating each other. Younger males, however, were frequently testing females to find out whether they were in heat. Coming up behind a female, a male nuzzled and sniffed her anal area, which stimulated her to urinate. The male then checked her urine, from its odor being able to ascertain the state of her estrus. Males sometimes importuned certain females so often that they ran out of urine.

On November 25, at 8:40 A.M., the bachelor herd suddenly broke up, the males crossing an icy stream to join a herd of females. The main rut had begun.

The rut lasts only a few weeks. With a male seldom having an opportunity to mate before the age of five years and seldom living as long as fifteen years, his whole reproductive life—his whole raison d'être—is crowded into but a few months of his existence. No wonder males seek their goals with such urgency.

A male approaches a female in a semi-crouch, his tongue flicking. When close to her, he may rotate his head sideways and deliver a gentle kick. More often than not the female trots aside. But when she is in heat she tolerates his advances and he remains with her. Occasionally she flees, and both then race wildly over the slopes, hurtling down precipices in a shower of stones. One would think that there would be selective advantage in courting with restraint on cliffs, yet bharal may at such times be quite reckless. Excited by seeing the chase, other males pursue the pair and try to horn in. A lunge by the dominant male may be enough to deter such ardent swains, but sometimes a male with even larger horns arrives and appropriates the female simply by halting broadside in front of her pursuer and blocking his access. Finally, the female may retreat onto some lofty ledge, where mating then occurs. By choosing such a precarious position, she effectively reduces competition among males, there seldom being room for more than one to maneuver.

Most adult males remained for days with the females in certain herds, waiting for a chance to mate. But a few of them roamed widely, actively searching among various herds for a female in heat. Sheep differ somewhat from bharal in that most adult rams move restlessly from herd to herd, seldom remaining for long with any females unless there is one in estrus. Male goats roam less than do bharal. These differences can be related to the social structure and, by extension, to the habitat of the species: herds of Eurasian sheep are widely and unpredictably scattered wherever there may be nutritious forage, and rams must therefore search for ewes; by contrast, goats live in fairly cohesive herds whose existence revolves around certain cliffs, and males have little need to wander. In this trait, as in various others, bharal are intermediate between sheep and goats.

Although the rut was exciting to watch, I realized that the behavior of bharal was much like that of other hoofed animals, that their courtship patterns had remained conservative in evolution. Although I wanted to observe the rut until the end, this was not feasible. Our food supply was nearly exhausted, and we had to supplement our rations by trading with the lama: an old pair of shoes for two pounds of potatoes; empty biscuit tins for rancid butter. Peter Matthiessen had already left with two companions who had earlier agreed to accompany him. They returned to Katmandu before the crisp November skies had given way to December storms. Snow clouds now scudded along the slopes, driven by bitter winds; soon all passes would be closed, and we would be trapped until spring. Yet even these few weeks had given me intriguing glimpses into bharal biology, and I had at least a tentative answer as to whether the species is a sheep or a goat.

Adult bharal males readily associate with females throughout the year, and in this respect they resemble goats. Only a few males roam during the rut, the animals being in this respect intermediate between sheep and goats. Males threaten each other directly by such means as lunging and clashing and, to a lesser extent, indirectly by displaying themselves broadside and otherwise. Sheep use more indirect aggression, and goats limit themselves almost wholly to the direct. Female bharal fight quite often, behaving like female goats and not like placid ewes. In general, bharal society seems goatlike, but with some sheeplike traits. I would surmise that the ancestors of bharal evolved on cliffs and that they later occupied less precipitous terrain, where new selection pressures modified their society in the direction characterized by sheep.

Turning to specific behavior patterns, one has to decide whether similar traits have developed independently in two species—that they evolved convergently—or whether they share a common origin. For example, both bharal and sheep rub as a friendly gesture. The part they rub is divergent—the former rub rumps, the latter faces—and the evolution of the behavior seems convergent. The huddle may be convergent, too, both habitats and societies having favored some means by which males can interact informally. There is a major difference in the way goats and sheep clash. Goats rear bolt upright and lunge downward onto the horns of an opponent. Bharal often fight like that too, even though they do not now live on cliffs, where this mode of fighting seems more sensible than the long rush practiced by sheep. Bharal mouth their penises like goats but they do not soak themselves with urine; thus they behave as if they were at an evolutionary stage prior to the one reached by goats.

The evidence indicates that bharal are basically goats. Some of their sheeplike traits can be ascribed to convergent evolution, the species having settled in a habitat usually occupied by sheep. This is more than merely a situation of behavior modified by change. Bharal remain rather generalized. Their horns are fairly short bashing instruments, not quite like those of either sheep or goats. In their glandular structure, in their use of the penis, and in other traits, bharal show an evolutionary hesitation to specialize—they have straddled an evolutionary fence. They could become either sheep or goats with only minor alterations, and if I had to design a hypothetical ancestor of these two forms it would look much like a bharal. Bharal probably split from goat stock shortly after the sheep and goats diverged from their common ancestor to develop along separate evolutionary paths.

It was our last morning at Shey. Sherpa Phu-Tsering sprinkled some incense into the embers of the juniper fire and scattered rice at the entrance of our hut to bring good luck on our journey. Bent under our packs, the four of us left Shey and headed eastward over a route different from the one that had brought us. After several hours we reached the top of a pass. Below us, a bearded vulture glided stiff-winged down the valley toward Shey. I watched until it disappeared among the wind-beaten summits, carrying with it my dream of a lost horizon.

A day later only one pass remained, a pass 17,500 feet high, before we could descend to the lowlands. The weather was ominous as we began the ascent, toiling in single file. Clouds engulfed us, and snow, driven by raging winds, clawed at us. Soon we were lost in a blizzard, able to see neither the route nor the direction of the pass. Then, above us, we heard bells ringing and men calling. And snaking down out of the whiteness came a trade caravan of sixty yaks. Encrusted with snow, the men and beasts plodded past and vanished as if they had never been. Within five minutes their tracks, too, were gone. But at intervals we now found frozen yak droppings; and using these trail markers, we continued our journey.

At the top of the pass was a stone cairn surmounted by a gnarled pole. Tattered prayer flags—or wind pictures, as the Tibetans call them—fluttered from the pole, tied there by travelers as offerings after having surmounted the pass. As we dipped over the crest into the valley beyond, I, too, gave my quiet thanks to the mountain gods.

[1977]

Tibetan Prairie Dogs

Pika

The black-lipped pika of the Tibetan uplands is a keystone species—that is, one that makes a major contribution to the functioning of the ecosystem. By digging burrows, this energetic and engaging relative of rabbits recycles nutrients, aerates the soil, increases plant diversity, and provides protected nest sites for a variety of small birds. Various flies pollinate flowers on these alpine steppes, and during the frequent summer snow- and windstorms the flies may seek shelter in pika burrows. Virtually all of the ecosystem's predators, from wolf and brown bear to saker falcon and upland hawk, depend on pikas as an important food source. But pikas eat grass and therefore are thought to compete with livestock for forage. Between 1986 and 1994 alone about 29,000 square miles of rangeland were poisoned to eradicate pikas. A common poison is zinc phosphide, which causes lingering disability and finally death. As with the poisoning of prairie dogs in the United States, the agencies involved have continued the practice long after it was shown to be outmoded and shortsighted.

I obtained only a general impression of pikas and their role in the ecosystem, but Andrew Smith and Marc Foggin have studied them in detail. In landscapes of lush meadow, a hundred pikas may crowd onto two to three acres, where they live in families consisting of an adult male, an adult female, and five to ten youngsters of at least two litters—all occupying one burrow system with many entrances.

The slope falls away before me to a plain beyond which smooth hills undulate to the horizon, no building, no road disrupting the immensity of the grasslands. A distant herd of dark animals could be bison. Somewhat nearer, the flash of a white rump draws my attention to a lone tan creature like a pronghorn antelope. Looking still more closely, I see many earthen mounds, each marking the site of a burrow, as in a vast prairie dog town.

Mine is not a vision of the past, of the American plains over a hundred years ago, but of northeastern Tibet at 14,000 feet today. Those dark forms are yaks, domestic descendants of wild ones that still roam the remote areas. The solitary animal is a Tibetan gazelle; and pikas, not prairie dogs, inhabit the burrows.

In North America, pikas live in talus and other rock wastes near or above timberline. Small and gray, they resemble chunky, tailless mice as they scurry around collecting grass to dry in the sun and then store

The diminutive black-lipped pika, a relative of rabbits, lives locally in huge colonies on the Tibetan plateau. Herders dislike the pika because they say it eats too much of the grass that should be reserved for livestock.

piled among rocks as winter food. However, like their relatives the rabbits and hares, pikas have adapted to various habitats. One species in western China lives in wet bamboo forests together with the giant panda. Another, known as the black-lipped pika, has settled on the Tibetan plains. It weighs four to five ounces, twice as much as the North American one, and is light brown rather than gray.

Since pikas and I are largely diurnal, we saw much of each other while I was on a wildlife survey in China's Qinghai Province, last July and August. On my entering a colony, the pikas ducked into their burrows, but if I stood still, heads quickly emerged again, shiny eyes judged my intentions, and the animals soon resumed their routine.

Life in a pika colony is hectic, even frantic, especially in the late afternoon. Pikas are tense, their movements nervous, their bodies prepared for action as they constantly monitor the terrain and each other. Most are busy foraging. They munch grasses and sedges, eating blades bottom-first. And they hurry along their runways with flowers in their mouths to store heaped at burrow entrances, the base of tussocks, and other protected sites.

Some stock their larder with only one kind of blossom, such as the flowering heads of polygonum. Others have flamboyant tastes, picking aster, lousewort, cinquefoil, poppy, sage, iris, thistle, gentian—a whole bouquet of purple, blue, white, yellow, and red. Pikas hoard little food in July, for heavy rains would spoil it. But just before a long sunny spell in August they harvest diligently. Can they forecast weather?

Geysers of earth often erupt from one or more holes as owners enlarge and clear tunnels. Once, in a fit of excess energy, I excavated a tunnel system to become familiar with a pika's domestic arrangements. I don't know who owned it, male or female, but probably the former, as the interior was spartan, without a cozy nest. There were three entrances and twenty-eight feet of zigzagging passageways, none more than a foot and a half below the surface. Some were connecting, others dead-end. One tunnel stopped abruptly a mere inch from the tunnel of a neighbor; the pikas carefully retained their privacy. At many bends the animal had scratched a small chamber that it used as a latrine. A total of fourteen such latrines kept the tunnels clean.

When not foraging or digging, pikas seem to bicker with neighbors. Two often rear up and pummel each other with forepaws. Trespassing young, grown and emigrating from their homes, are constantly harassed. I particularly remember one tattered youngster. An adult bit it in the neck, then chased it. To escape, it rushed into a burrow but just as rapidly raced out, pursued by the irate owner. Overtaken, it pressed itself motionless to the ground in submission, a gesture that saved it from further punishment. I last saw it at another burrow entrance, hunched nervously, its tenancy uncertain.

The pikas' preference for gentle, well-drained land in which to dig burrows and live together in large colonies reminded me of prairie dogs. Indeed, pikas on the Tibetan plains occupy the same ecological niche as prairie dogs once did on the North American plains. The two even have the same enemy. Once, sitting in front of my tent with my breakfast bowl of rice porridge in hand, I spotted a lithe, dark creature emerging from a burrow at the heels of a pika. Within a second both vanished back into the earth, where somehow the pika escaped. The weasel-like animal reappeared undeterred, glided into another burrow, flushed out a pika, and grabbed it by the scruff. Head held high, the predator carried its trophy to a nearby den. Now, for the first time, I saw its black-masked face: a ferret—*Mustela eversmannii*. It emerged again and, ignoring me, rapidly entered two burrows in succession without making a kill, then appeared from a third carrying a limp pika by the back.

The black-footed ferret of North America, a close relative of this one, is nearly extinct, only about 130 surviving in a small area of Wyoming and perhaps a few in South Dakota and Montana. The black-footed ferret's drastic decline has one principal cause. Its prey consists mainly of prairie dogs, and prairie dogs eat grass, all of which ranchers claim vociferously for their cattle and sheep. With simpleminded dedication, prairie dogs have been and are still being poisoned by ranchers and agents of the United States government. The black-footed ferret died in

*The steppe polecat (*Mustela eversmannii*), a relative of the American ferret, preys on pikas, as do mammalian predators such as the brown bear, wolf, Tibetan fox, lynx, and Tibetan sand fox, as well as many raptors from the saker falcon to the upland hawk.*

the burrows along with the prairie dogs. But such dismal matters are surely of no concern to ferrets and pikas in remote Tibet.

One noon I climbed up toward a limestone massif. Rumpled hills extended to the horizon, except to the south, where they broke against snow mountains. A bearded vulture rode the updrafts along shimmering cliffs, and from far below, where the Gangtsa monastery is barely visible in the folds of the hills, rose the sonorous tones of two horns. I should have felt exhilarated climbing into space with music of an ancient culture suspended around me to give human measure to this vastness, yet I was troubled; something seemed amiss.

Then I realized there were no pikas. The many burrows I had passed lacked fresh earth at the entrances. The droppings in the outdoor latrines were dry, without luster, and the hay piles were sodden, uncared for. I was in a city of the dead, a Pompeii where a catastrophe abruptly had terminated the flow of life. Had it been a virulent disease, a mass exodus? On returning to camp, I told my Chinese coworkers about the pikas.

"They have been poisoned with zinc phosphide," explained an official of the wildlife department.

My first thought was, surely not near a monastery. Buddhist religion forbids the unnecessary taking of life, any life. Aloud, I asked, "Why?"

One of the Chinese scientists replied: "Pikas are bad." When I looked startled, he continued: "They eat the grass, which yaks and sheep need."

"It is true that pikas eat grass, but they also eat many herbs that livestock do not like. Some of these herbs are poisonous," I replied, pointing at both *Stellaria* and *Ligularia* in flower all around us.

Not deterred by my reply, the scientist added: "And pikas cause erosion by digging burrows."

I swept my arm toward the nearby slopes, where innumerable livestock trails cut deeply into the thin sod layer, forming erosion terraces, and where landslips exposed sterile rock. I responded: "Pikas like to live in overgrazed habitat, because they can burrow easily in erosion terraces, and because herbs provide ample food. Poor livestock management, not pikas, caused this erosion."

"Tibetans tell me that a horse may break its leg when it steps into a burrow," asserted the scientist, presenting the third and last argument in his case against pikas.

I did not reply. Exactly the same three explanations have been given to excuse the wanton eradication of America's prairie dogs. These rodents, too, eat noxious herbs and colonize habitats overgrazed by livestock. And, of course, North American rangelands continue to deteriorate, without there being many prairie dogs left to blame.

Later I collected forty-eight pika food plants, eleven of them grasses and sedges and thirty-seven of them herbs. Tibet's livestock and pikas obviously compete somewhat for the same resources, but by eating herbs, pikas may slow the spread of plants not palatable to livestock and thus improve conditions for grasses.

Pikas no doubt also benefit the grasslands in subtler ways. The underground latrines must add valuable nutrients to the soil. Hume's ground jay—a pert tan-and-white bird—nests in pika burrows. Deprived of these, it will surely decline, with unknown long-term effects.

Is the history of America's rangelands to be repeated in Tibet? In spite of vastly different educational backgrounds, many American ranchers and Tibetan herdsmen give the same imperceptive reasons to justify an ecologically illiterate action. In both countries education has failed to sharpen perceptions, to teach how to doubt and seek understanding, to instill a sense of wonder in the natural world. Both literally and metaphorically, I felt like a lone ecological voice crying in the wilderness.

So far, the pikas of the Tibetan Plateau have suffered less than the larger mammals. The wild yak, Tibetan wild ass, chiru, and wolf have vanished from populated areas, and the big Tibetan sheep and brown bear almost so. Only species difficult to hunt have been able to coexist with herders in certain localities. Devoted to life among cliffs, blue sheep remain the most abundant large wild herbivores. And where blue sheep are common, snow leopards also persist, although in low numbers. White-lipped deer now occur mainly in several forest tracts along the eastern edge of the plateau, where trees or shrubs provide protective cover. Fleetness and sharp eyesight have saved a few Tibetan gazelles on the plains.

Fortunately, large stretches of the Tibetan Plateau remain undeveloped and unpopulated; these retain their future. Determined to conserve its natural resources, China is making an inventory of Tibet's wildlife and is establishing reserves. In 1983, the snow leopard received full legal protection in the same category as the giant panda and the black-necked crane.

North America lost its Great Plains herds, but Tibet's can survive in the bleak western highlands where humankind has as yet found little reason to settle, though mining and oil exploration may soon change this. It is in these highlands that the Chinese government can assure wildlife the protection and space it needs to roam unfettered over the roof of the world.

[1985]

In a High and
Sacred Realm

Chiru

In the Chang Tang, those austere and wild uplands of the Tibetan Plateau, all is silence and light, horizon gives way to horizon, and the starry sky seems wider and deeper than elsewhere. My involvement there began in 1985 and continues still. Somehow I cannot cease traveling over that sweeping steppe and working on behalf of its wild yaks, chiru (or Tibetan antelope, as they are also called), and other wildlife.

Since the early 1990s the Chinese government has established two major protected areas adjoining the Chang Tang Reserve, the Kekexili in 1995 and the Mid-Kunlun in 2001—the former in Qinghai Province and the latter in Xinjiang. Altogether about 175,000 square miles of the ecosystem had a measure of protection, a tremendous achievement by China. In addition, I promoted creating a final protected area for a major calving ground of chiru, whose story is so well told in Rick Ridgeway's book The Big Open. In 2006, Xinjiang established this area as the West Kunlun Reserve to further assure the wildlife a future.

Chiru continue to be killed for their fine wool, which is smuggled to Kashmir to be woven into expensive shahtoosh shawls, but greater enforcement efforts and publicity in China, India, the United States, and other countries have reduced this illicit trade. No adequate census of chiru numbers has ever been made, though when I returned in 2003 to survey wildlife in an area I had *also surveyed a decade earlier, I found to my delight that chiru, as well as the wild yak and Tibetan wild ass, had increased there.*

But in the years between these surveys, a drastic change in government policy eliminated communal grazing areas and gave each household a parcel of land on which to manage its domestic sheep, goats, and yaks. Will nomads now overstock and degrade the rangelands? Will they tolerate wildlife that competes with livestock for food? Cultures change constantly. The challenge is to promote harmonious coexistence between wildlife and nomads with their livestock. This includes encouraging people to retain their spiritual values, without which conservation may not persist.

Nearly two thousand chiru flowed over the curve of a hill. Pale and insubstantial in the heat waves, they streamed toward me, the murmur of their soft grunts filling the air. There were only females and young. Whenever a mother briefly halted to forage, her month-old offspring suckled quickly or bedded down, exhausted.

In June the pregnant females had hurried north, moving silently over shimmering plains and past snow-swept mountains, following an ancient migration route to some mysterious place to give birth. It is a place so remote that even nomadic herdsmen do not venture near it. It is so bleak that the animals find little more than the dry leaves of a sharp-tipped sedge to eat. We had tried to follow the herds, but severe blizzards stopped us at Heishi Beihu, "blackrock northlake," so named for its black lava flows. Now, in early August, the chiru were a hundred miles south on their return migration.

As the animals approached, I became a motionless mound, my face tucked among cushions of edelweiss, yellow-flowered cinquefoil, and tufts of feather grass. We were at 16,500 feet. Behind me glacier-flanked peaks of the Aru Range rose abruptly, several over 20,000 feet in elevation, and on my left was Luotuo Hu, "camel lake," turquoise and tranquil among brown, rumpled hills. The chiru, normally so shy,

The Chang Tang (Tibetan for "northern plain") is a vast upland that spans Tibet and Qinghai Province and one of the last great strongholds of Central Asian wildlife, including chiru. Here, a herd migrates in search of forage after a heavy snowstorm in October 1985, which caused the starvation of many chiru and other animals.

surrounded me, some at less than a hundred feet, as they leisurely headed down valley. Another herd came, and another. Only about half the females had young at heel, as compared to two-thirds with young at this season two years before. The June blizzards had probably killed many newborns.

I felt becalmed in time and space. In 1903 the British explorer Capt. C.G. Rawling had also witnessed this great migration: "Almost from my feet away to the north and east, as far as the eye could reach, were thousands upon thousands of doe antelope with their young. . . . [T]here could not have been less than 15,000 or 20,000 visible at one time."

Rawling was the last Westerner to observe this spectacle until my wife, Kay, and I visited the Aru area in 1988 and again in 1990 and 1992. There are fewer chiru now, and the groups we observed belong to the largest of the four known migratory populations in the Chang Tang, Tibetan for "northern plain." These unhampered migrations indicate that the Chang Tang harbors a rare treasure, an undamaged ecosystem, a truly wild land not yet controlled by humankind.

The Tibetan Plateau is about 950,000 square miles in size, and about 70 percent of this area consists of high pastures. The highest of these is the Chang Tang; it spreads over much of the western and northern parts of the Tibet Autonomous Region of the People's Republic of China and also extends east into neighboring Qinghai Province and north into the Xinjiang Autonomous Region as far as the Kunlun Mountains, which trace the northern rim of the Tibetan Plateau. Pastoralists have long settled the good grazing lands of the Chang Tang. But the desolate northern area, north of about 32° N latitude, has remained either uninhabited or only sparsely populated. This section covers some 200,000 square miles, an area larger than California or Germany, and most lies between 15,000 and 17,000 feet in elevation. It is a harsh landscape of forbidding grandeur and infinite horizons. Winds rage, their force broken by neither trees nor shrubs. Winter temperatures drop to −40°F, and even in summer the night temperatures hover around freezing.

At the turn of the century, the Swedish explorer Sven Hedin traveled for fifty-five days across the Chang Tang without seeing another person. He wrote: "Roads! There are no other paths there than those beaten out by wild yaks." As a boy I had read Hedin's accounts. The Chang Tang became to me a fabled land of dreams and adventures. And later, after I became a naturalist, the area retained its sense of unknown possibilities, with its fauna of Tibetan wild asses, known locally as kiang, of wild yaks, of huge-horned Tibetan argali sheep, and other species, all still unstudied. Here one can step beyond the known world back in time to explore where no outsider has ever trod.

Another chiru herd passed by me, and then the slopes were silent. I climbed uphill toward my waiting car, almost afloat in the hard, bright light. Overhead a flock of sand grouse and a few white clouds were on the wing, and the sky was as blue as a poppy. Nine kiang, elegant in their russet and white coats, ascended a slope opposite me, a stallion at the rear. Many stallions are solitary during the summer rut, hoping that a herd of mares will wander into their territory. The belly of one mare

The chiru shares its spartan habitat with other wild ungulates including the Tibetan gazelle, the rare wild yak, and the Tibetan wild ass, or kiang (shown here). During winter the kiang may gather in herds of 250 or more, a magnificent sight.

bulged; she would give birth within days. Four wild yak bulls grazed on a far hillside, looking huge and rugged even at a distance.

Ahead of me, stretching to the south, was the Aru basin, about seven hundred square miles in extent. The Chang Tang consists mostly of lake basins without outlets, separated by bald ridges and mountain chains. No great rivers have carved through this terrain except at the eastern margin, where the Yangtze River has its source. As glaciers melted after the last ice age, vast lakes filled the basins. The land became increasingly drier and lakes grew smaller, some disappearing. Old beach lines can be seen as much as 600 feet above present lake levels. Today the region is a high-altitude desert with only about five to ten inches of precipitation a year, most as snow and hail in the summer. With a drop in lake levels, minerals were concentrated, making most water brackish or saline, undrinkable. Once one large lake filled the Aru basin; now it is divided into two smaller lakes, Aru Co—*co* means lake in Tibetan—and Memar Co, near which we had our camp.

Our expedition leader, Gu Binyuan of the Tibet Plateau Institute of Biology in Lhasa, waited for me by the car. Distances in the Chang Tang are so vast and the terrain so remote that it is best to use four-wheel-drive vehicles. Most areas are accessible, especially in winter, when the soil is dry and streams are frozen. But I preferred to walk: one can only make intimate contact with an area on foot, roofless, exposed to the raw bite of wind. Besides, the animals of the Chang Tang are not innocent of cars. Wild yaks may travel for miles and chiru seek the horizon with dazzling speed when they perceive a vehicle, obviously aware that death can follow.

Once when walking far north of the Aru basin, we met a lynx in a desolate place where the plains are as gray and corrugated as a yak chip. The land was empty, with little grass and few animals; an occasional gray-rumped Tibetan woolly hare—a species unique to the plateau—huddled in a shallow scrape. No humans came to this isolated spot. But the lynx had settled here. At rest on a cliff, he apparently thought us inconse-quential; there was not even fire in his eyes as he gazed in our direction.

In the Aru basin a Tibetan gazelle, a lone female, fled from our car with stiff-legged bounds, her white rump patch flashing like a helio-graph. Perhaps she had her offspring cached nearby. Weighing only about thirty pounds, these delicate and swift animals are the most wide-spread of the wild ungulates on the grass steppes; they are usually seen in small herds of up to a dozen individuals. Farther on, the plains sud-denly rippled, and dust rose as if swept by wind. My scope revealed a herd of male chiru, about 350 of them, racing several abreast, their horns as erect as the lances of a company of knights. Perhaps they had scented a wolf—two packs roamed the basin—or perhaps they merely feared the car. Males, unlike females, do not troop as far as two hundred miles to the barren north in spring. Instead most migrate only partway and loiter the summer away alone or in herds. By November they will have rejoined the females in preparation for the rut.

I had come to the Chang Tang to chronicle the obscure lives of the plateau's large predators (snow leopard, wolf, lynx, Tibetan brown bear) and six wild ungulates (wild yak, kiang, blue sheep, Tibetan argali, gazelle, and chiru). I was interested in their status and distribution, birth and death rates, food habits, movements. The chiru became my special focus. Just as the seasonal wanderings of the wildebeest define the ecosystem of the Serengeti in Tanzania, so do the travels of chiru in the Chang Tang. Between 1985 and 1987, before beginning work in Tibet, I had surveyed wildlife in those parts of the Chang Tang that extend into Qinghai and Xinjiang. Large tracts had little or no wildlife, and those animals that survived seemed living elegies for a past that was rapidly vanishing. Would the mystery, solitude, and inspiration of the Chang Tang be marred by the extermination of its noble animals and the construction of roads, mining camps, and other development? The 17,300-square-mile Arjin Shan reserve had recently been established in Xinjiang at the northern edge of the Chang Tang, a notable action by China, but it was not enough. I was reminded of the last words of Milarepa, a Tibetan hermit who died in 1123:

> Do if you like that which may seem sinful
> But help living beings,
> Because that is truly pious work.

Conservation initiatives are too often made after wildlife has been decimated and habitat modified; I was determined to help the Chang Tang endure as part of Tibet's natural heritage. By 1992, while we were in the Aru basin, a responsive Tibet Autonomous Region government was in the final stages of establishing a Chang Tang Reserve. China subsequently made it a national reserve. Approximately 115,500 square miles in size—six hundred miles at its longest and three hundred miles at its widest—the Chang Tang Reserve is the second largest in the world, exceeded only by Greenland National Park, which consists mostly of ice cap.

Our camp—a cook tent, four small sleeping tents, and the vehicles drawn close as windbreaks—was tucked against a hill beside a glacial stream. On our return, I told Kay jubilantly about my day with the chiru. And she showed me plants she had pressed for identification, a tiny polygonum, a purple-flowered legume, a matlike composite—inconspicuous or procumbent, as if reticent about facing the harsh environment.

Black-lipped pikas—small, tailless relatives of rabbits—had burrows within a few feet of our tent. Kay had been observing their nose-to-nose greetings and playful boxing, and she kept notes on their behavior. Pikas are an essential link in the food chain of the Chang Tang. Upland hawks, saker falcons, and sand foxes subsist on them, brown bears dig them from their burrows, and wolves snatch them up when larger prey is unavailable. On the lush pastures of eastern Qinghai, each pika family—a male, female, and their offspring—lives in an extensive burrow system. But here on the spartan uplands, where most of the ground is bare and food widely dispersed, pikas use scattered simple burrows, each six to ten feet long, and scuttle between them.

Hume's ground jays, small tan birds with curved bills, were feeding nestlings in an abandoned pika burrow near our tent. "Three adults have been bringing insects to the nest all day," Kay said. This nest had not just

A male chiru paws snow away in search of sparse forage.

a pair of adults but a third adult helper, probably a fledgling from the previous year.

Chi Doa, a Tibetan who was second in command on our trip, called *chi fan*—dinner. We sat on boxes and water cans outside the cook tent, each of us with a bowl of noodles and canned peas spiced with red pepper. Yak chips smoldered, heating water for tea.

The Aru Range glowed in sunset hues of sepia and gunmetal gray. Dawa, one of our drivers, enthusiastically told us that he had spotted a large herd of wild yaks in the nearby foothills earlier that day. Perhaps we could find them again tomorrow. The cold hit hard as soon as the sun vanished behind the ranges. Kay and I retreated to our mountain tent, where, tucked into our sleeping bag, we read a little by flashlight. Before going to sleep, I looked outside. There were stars close and bright but also a cloud bank that spoke of snow. Later, snow came, rustling as soft as moth wings on our tent.

Millions of domestic yaks inhabit Central Asia. Essential to the lives of many people, yaks provide meat, wool, and milk rich in butterfat, as well as fuel and transport. But to have a true image of the yak, one must meet a wild bull in unrestricted freedom. A ton of power with imposing thirty-inch horns, the wind whipping his long mantle of hair, he takes possession of the landscape. Wild yaks were once abundant on the Tibetan Plateau. During his travels in eastern Qinghai in 1889, William Rockhill found hills "literally black with yak; they could be seen by the thousands."

Those plains are now empty of yaks, killed off for meat since the 1950s, when a new road made the area accessible to hunters. This species of wild cattle is now largely confined to the most remote parts of the Chang Tang, and even there it is becoming increasingly scarce. Herds of twenty or thirty or even a hundred wild yaks can still be seen, as can bulls, singly and in small groups. In one uninhabited area of 3,200 square miles we found just seventy-three yaks during an intensive survey. The Aru basin and area surrounding it were exceptional in that they had, to my knowledge, the largest remaining concentration of wild yaks in Tibet, about one thousand.

The next day we found the herd that Dawa had reported. The yaks rested on dun slopes the sun had already freed of snow. From a great distance I could count over two hundred black dots speckling the hill-side—and two golden dots. Wild yaks are typically a lustrous black except for a flush of gray on the muzzle. But in the Aru region a star-tling mutation has occurred: 1 to 2 percent of the yaks are completely golden. A black female may have a golden calf or a golden female a black calf.

Most of the yaks drowsed in ponderous ease. At the edge of the herd, a bull trailed a cow closely, guarding her from other bulls; the rut had begun, and she would give birth eight and a half months later.

A short distance from the others a herd of forty yaks grazed placidly on the plain. Suddenly the animals bunched and bolted. Five lanky wolves surged around and through the herd. After a headlong rush the yaks halted, then stood indecisively. Occasionally a wolf swept closely past the herd or a yak made a token rush with lowered horns. It was a standoff. The wolves apparently were searching for calves, but there were none. Soon the pack bounded off to join a sixth wolf on a nearby rise; the yaks lingered before drifting toward the hills.

After observing the yaks a while, I too wandered off. As usual I remained alert for brown bears. The Tibetan brown bear, a subspecies found only on the plateau and now the rarest large mammal there, has black legs, a broad, white collar, shaggy ears, and an irascible temper. Near here a bear had rushed from a depression with her head threaten-ingly low, hair bristling, and with utter fury she pursued the car in which Kay was traveling. The animal revealed its wildness, and Kay was suit-ably impressed.

"I have never, ever, seen such an angry animal," she told me later. It was a female accompanied by two cubs.

If this account tarries so long in the Aru basin, it is because wild hoofed animals are almost always in view and because no area of the

Female chiru migrate to remote calving grounds in desolate regions uninhabited by nomads, where they give birth together. Then they migrate back to better pastures, a long trek for the newborns. Here a month-old calf suckles.

Chang Tang has so imprinted itself on my memory. With its ecological wholeness and stark beauty, its mysterious horizons and unfettered freedom, the Aru basin is a place where both body and mind can travel; it represents to me the spiritual essence of Tibet.

In 1891 Hamilton Bower, an officer in the British Army, visited Aru Co and wrote afterward: "In every direction antelope and yak in incredible numbers were seen, some grazing, some lying down. No trees, no signs of man, and this peaceful-looking lake, never before seen by a European eye, seemingly given over as a happy grazing ground to the wild animals." Now, a century later, wildlife is still abundant here, more so than in any other place I saw in the Chang Tang.

The Aru Range provides fresh water and with it good grazing. But the growing season is short, a mere three months, and for most of the year the herbivores are forced to feed on dry, dead plants that are not very nutritious. Only some thirty plant species provide most of their forage. Yet the animals have divided their sparse resources with harmony and simplicity. For instance, blue sheep favor the vicinity of cliffs, wild yaks and argali sheep the foothills and high rolling terrain, and others the plains. Kiang are partial to eating feather grass, whereas chiru sample a wide variety of plants, from coarse sedges to succulent legumes.

My Chinese and Tibetan coworkers were mostly from the Tibet Plateau Institute of Biology and the Tibet Forest Bureau. Over a period of several years we made five journeys through the Chang Tang Reserve, each lasting one to three months. Our work was made possible by these two Tibetan organizations, the Wildlife Conservation Society, and the National Geographic Society. Driving cross-country, the land expanded before us, scoured by wind, immense and vital in its solitude, our vehicles providing the only human measure. We usually traveled with two cars plus a truck that carried fuel and food. One car would lead, selecting a route over hills, through ravines, around soft ground, and the heavily laden truck brought up the rear. If we misjudged the terrain, we or the truck often got stuck axle deep in mud. This could require a day or more of digging, excellent exercise at 16,000 feet. Permafrost underlies much of the northern Chang Tang at a depth of two to three feet, but the surface could be so sodden after days of summer storms that we could not travel. I would have preferred pack animals to vehicles. There is atavistic pleasure in traversing these uplands in the simple fashion of another age. We did this only once, for three weeks, riding on Bactrian camels at the leisurely pace determined by the animals themselves. But time was short, our mission urgent.

A mere dozen or so Western expeditions had penetrated what is now the Chang Tang Reserve before we began our collaborative work there. We sometimes crossed the routes of these early travelers. In 1889 Prince Henry of Orleans and Gabriel Bonvalot were the first to cross the area north to south, and Hamilton Bower first went west to east in 1891. St. George Littledale's caravan in 1895 included his wife and terrier. Sven Hedin made three journeys, the last one from 1906 to 1908, and with it the period of foreign exploration there came to an end. Most of these expeditions were attempting to reach Lhasa, the holy sanctuary of Tibetan Buddhism, by entering forbidden Tibet through the uninhabited Chang Tang. All failed. Tibetan soldiers posted near Siling Co and other places turned the expeditions aside.

The area saw no more foreigners until 1950. That year Frank Bessac, an American Fulbright scholar; Douglas Mackiernan, the American consul in Xinjiang's capital, Urumqi; and three White Russians fled the civil war in Xinjiang and tried to reach India by crossing the Tibetan Plateau. They had struggled almost across the Chang Tang when nervous Tibetan border guards shot Mackiernan and two of the White Russians. But Bessac and one companion survived to be safely escorted to Lhasa and on to India.

Since the 1960s a number of Chinese scientific expeditions have conducted research in the region, but until recent years the accounts of early Western travelers provided our only information about the wildlife. Some wrote perceptively; others viewed animals in terms of recipes or provided erroneous insights, as when the British wanderer Henry Savage Landor wrote about the kiang: "Their apparent tameness is often deceptive, enabling them to draw quite close to the unwary traveler, and then with a sudden dash seize him by the stomach."

Like some early travelers, we found that wildlife was not evenly distributed throughout the Chang Tang. For miles we might see nothing except perhaps a lone kiang on a ridge, his tail blowing, the sky to himself, or perhaps a glint of gazelles. Then suddenly in the empty land we would come upon an aggregation of animals where grazing was especially good. Overall the average density was less than one animal per square mile. The northern half of the reserve is desolate, with gazelles almost absent, argalis as rare there as elsewhere, chiru seasonal, and the other animals few and scattered. The region remains unpopulated because livestock cannot easily subsist there. By contrast the southern half of the reserve with its grass steppes is critical to the survival of the wildlife. Here the chiru gather by the thousands for the winter; here the kiang may still roam in herds of one hundred or even twice that. But almost gone from the south is the totem of the Chang Tang, the wild yak.

Once only a few pastoralists used these grasslands seasonally, if at all. They herded their sheep and goats and yaks, and they hunted for subsistence. In 1906, for example, Sven Hedin came across a tent inhabited by a woman with three children. "She had arrived from Gertse [Gerze] seventeen days before with her two husbands, who had returned to Gertse after they had filled her tent for her with wild-ass meat. She owned a few yaks and a small flock of sheep and would live for the next three months on game—yaks, kiang, and antelopes." Tibetan pastoralists hunted wolves, lynx, foxes, and bears for their pelts and to protect livestock. And a small amount of chiru wool was traded to India, where it was marketed as *shahtoosh,* the king of wool, because none finer exists. Such subsistence hunting by a few herdsmen with muzzle-loaders and traps had no measurable impact on the wildlife.

Indeed, hunters have been part of the Chang Tang for thousands of years. One day as I meandered far from camp along the beach of an ancient lake, its waters long ago transformed to dry steppe, I spied at my feet a sliver of stone, a piece of chert. Its charcoal color contrasted with the pale sand and pebbles around it. I picked it up. It was a stone tool, a flake with one edge chipped to make a cutting blade. Hunters had once camped here, perhaps five thousand years ago, perhaps ten thousand years.

All the way home I held the stone tool tightly in my hand, making human contact over the millennia with those who had also walked these unbounded uplands. And now that I had learned to see, I found stone tools in several localities, all good campsites, such as at the mouth of valleys and at hot springs. Most tools were scrapers or knives or microblades, tiny sharp flakes that can be hafted as arrowheads. The tool kit of a hunter.

Stone-tool sites extend far north into areas of the Chang Tang that are not inhabited today. Pollen analysis of lake sediment by researchers

With economic conditions improving, the lifestyle of nomads is changing from a
yak-hair tent to a more permanent base in a hut, and from horse to motorcycle.
But nomads continue to depend on their flocks of sheep, goats, and yaks for food
and for income from wool, milk products, and hides.

Huang Cixuan and Liang Yulian of the Chinese Academy of Sciences
shows that about five thousand to thirteen thousand years ago the
region was warmer and wetter than today. Then as now, most of the
Chang Tang consisted of steppe, but there were also stands of pine and
fir and thickets of tamarisk, willow, and alder. Lakes were then much
larger, and mountains bristled with glaciers. People and tents would
have been part of that landscape as well, and I now viewed it with a
sense of times past.

During recent decades the economy of pastoralists has changed.
Once families made long annual treks by yak caravan to trade wool, butter, and other products for such basic supplies as *tsampa*, the roasted
ground barley that is a Tibetan staple. But now trucks reach almost all
tent camps, even those of pastoralists who have moved north into the

Chang Tang to the limit of good grazing. The traditional system of pastoralism, which shifts livestock seasonally, has maintained the grasslands well; I saw no serious overgrazing in the reserve. Wildlife and livestock can obviously continue to coexist. However, with a ready access to markets, some pastoralists are now less tolerant of wild animals, especially kiang, which are thought to compete with livestock for food. Others still find quiet pleasure in their natural heritage. As one herdsman told me, "I like to see wild animals around."

With the advent of a cash economy, commercial hunting has been added to subsistence hunting. Wild yaks, with so much meat, were the first to be killed in great numbers. Officials from one town ventured far to the north into uninhabited terrain each autumn to shoot wild yaks by the truckload. We found yak heads littering the most remote areas. In 1988, in the small town of Gerze, I saw herdsmen plucking wool from chiru hides to sell to local dealers. In the courtyard of one such dealer were sacks of wool ready for smuggling into western Nepal and from there to Kashmir, where the wool is woven into scarves and shawls.

Since the mid-1980s the trade in such goods has become so lucrative that it has sharply driven up the price of chiru wool. In 1992 a herdsman received the equivalent of about $50 for a hide (the price of four sheep). But in Europe a small shawl sells for as much as $3,000 and a large one for $8,500 or more.

In the winter of 1991 we visited a hunting camp, one of four in a small area. There were three men, wrapped in sheepskin cloaks, from Gerze, more than 130 miles away. They had traveled here by yak caravan, leaving their other livestock and families behind. During the previous ten days they had trapped twenty-two chiru. The hides were stacked in their tent, the frozen bodies outside; they had also saved the heads of males, because the horns are widely used in traditional medicine and find a ready market in Lhasa and Beijing.

To catch chiru, the men used an ingenious circular foot trap with small pointed sticks projecting toward the center. The trap is placed on a trail over a hollow, concealed, and tied to a stake. When a chiru or

Left: *Tibetan nomads have traditionally hunted wildlife for subsistence. Here an infant lies in a cradle made from the hide of Tibetan wild ass, or kiang.*
Right: *My Tibetan coworker Dawa holds a handful of chiru hair and wool. The chiru is snared or shot and the wool plucked from its hide, then illegally exported to Kashmir, where it is woven into expensive* shahtoosh *shawls for the international market.*

gazelle steps into the trap and tries to withdraw its leg, the sticks dig into the skin, holding the animal.

Wild yaks and chiru are fully protected in China, and the Tibet Forest Bureau has tried to curtail the illegal wool trade. One truck driver, for example, was taken to court for killing three hundred chiru. However, control is extremely difficult, in part because officials, instead of upholding the laws, themselves often hunt. Most hunting is done by herdsmen, not usually by the capable ones whose flocks thrive but by those who have somehow failed, whose existence has become marginal. It is a difficult social problem that must be resolved.

In the past, the Aru basin was used by pastoralists only seasonally, usually for two to three months between May and September. To my consternation, five families with about forty people moved permanently into the basin in 1991, for one purpose only: to hunt chiru. One day we drove to the tent in which the headman of these families lived with his wife. We sat on a rug by the central stone and clay stove. He offered us salted tea; we bargained with him for a sheep, wanting to add fresh meat to our diet of rice and noodles and *tsampa*. I gave him a card, as I do to all herdsmen during these travels. On one side it has a drawing of the Buddhist saint Milarepa amid peaceful animals and of a kneeling hunter who has laid down his arms: a sword, a bow, a quiver of arrows. On the other side is one of Buddha's sayings in Tibetan script:

All beings tremble at punishment,
To all life is dear.
Comparing others to oneself,
One should neither kill nor cause to kill.

The herdsman reverently touched the card to his head and then placed it on the family shrine with its butter lamps and picture of the Dalai Lama. He told us, with Dawa translating into Chinese, that he was sixty-eight years old. His father and grandfather had lived in this region before him. The five families here owned a total of only about six hundred sheep and goats and forty-five yaks—and a truck.

How could they afford to buy a truck when they owned so little livestock? By killing chiru. And now more must be killed to buy gasoline for the truck. According to this man, vehicles with officials had come here from Gerze on two occasions the previous winter to hunt yaks and chiru with modern weapons.

"If the officials obey the law and stop hunting, we will, too," he said.

The pastoralists in the reserve should be allowed to continue their traditional lives. But if unrestricted commercial hunting continues, the wild yaks, chiru, and others will within a few years be reduced to tragic remnants. The fate of the bison on the American plains comes to mind.

Om Mani Padme Hum. This is the Tibetan invocation for the salvation of all living beings. To Tibetans life is holy, and the Chang Tang is a sacred realm. When the last wild yak has died and roads have been pushed to the rim of that remote world, Tibet will have been denatured, it will have lost something vital.

The high Chang Tang represents life at the edge, so precarious that wildlife cannot absorb the additional pressure of heavy hunting. On October 17, 1985, the most severe blizzard in thirty years covered the eastern Chang Tang with a foot of snow. Wind and sun usually clear away such snow, but this time it was calm and cold. At night, in our tent, the thermometer registered –25°F. The plains and distant white ranges, veiled by mist, had an Arctic aura. The wild hoofed animals had to paw through crusted snow for nourishment, and soon they were starving.

The dainty gazelles, trudging knee-deep through snow, suffered most. Exhausted, they reclined never to rise again, and in the great silence the snow drifted against their cold bodies. The lower legs of kiang became abraded and bloody from the frozen crust. Being large, kiang expended less energy in digging for food, and they survived the storm better than the gazelles and chiru. Many hundreds of chiru died of starvation, mainly females and young; we found 193 bodies in just one valley. Herds moved far afield from their usual wintering grounds, but they could not escape the icy grip on the land.

The blizzard had occurred not long before the onset of the rut. The surviving females were in such poor physical condition that they did not breed, or at least, very few had young with them when I returned the following year to check. This one blizzard drastically reduced the chiru population in the eastern Chang Tang and virtually eliminated two years of reproduction. Livestock suffered, too: the pastoralists lost two-thirds of their sheep and half their yaks. Both wild and domestic hoofed animals traditionally increase in number during good years, only to be reduced by such unpredictable catastrophes.

The chiru looks like an antelope and acts like an antelope—but it isn't one. George Amato, a conservation geneticist with the Wildlife Conservation Society, analyzed its mitochondrial DNA and found that the animal's closest evolutionary affinities are with sheep, goats, and their relatives. To discover what traits this so-called antelope shares with its sheep relatives or with the antelope and gazelles, I had to observe its behavior in detail. The December rut, when animals are most active, is the best time to do this. The eighty-pound males are then at their most handsome; their pale brown summer coat has changed to a light gray and white nuptial pelage, except that the face and front of the legs are black. A walnut-size bulge, a nasal sac, projects from the side of each nostril, giving the muzzle a swollen appearance. Chiru tend to aggregate at certain sites during the rut, in groups of a hundred or two hundred but sometimes more than a thousand.

One day I stood on a rise, eye to my scope, focused on chiru on the plain below. A male chased another full tilt for more than half a mile, puffs of dust exploding under their hoofs. I marveled at their stamina at these altitudes. And I also noted that my eyeballs were freezing. When I used the hand that had steadied the tripod and scope to thaw my face, the wind whipped the tripod away.

But there were also calm, warm days with temperatures around zero. One such day I walked among the chiru and sat down, quiet and immobile as a rock cairn. The animals soon forgot me. Males trotted past with heads held low and the white flag of their tails raised, as they gave primordial bellows, challenging other males, their nasal sacs acting as resonators.

If females wandered near a male, he herded them with muzzle skyward, showing off his white neck. Usually the females ignored him, but sometimes one bolted and was pursued by him. And during his absence another male might appropriate the remaining females.

A male does not defend a plot of land but instead tries to maintain a small harem for a few hours, just long enough for a female to come into heat. If a female is receptive, the male high-steps close behind her, bellows, and kicks the air with a stiff foreleg. He mounts by standing bolt upright, barely touching her—behavior typical of gazelles. This and some other behaviors suggest that chiru may be living relics of a line going back to the time when the true antelope and gazelles split from the sheep and goats during the Miocene, eight or more million years ago.

But such knowledge ceased to entice me that day, for the plain stretched into the sun's blinding light to a horizon of white hills aloof in their barrenness. A herdsman's tent huddled in the fold of the hills. A wolf strolled along a distant cutbank, and a flock of horned larks twittered by. And all around, the chiru danced on the tawny grass in their ancient ritual.

I was at the center of this sacred space, watching and aware, celebrating the harmonious balance of a fleeting moment. I was in a special place, as stated so well in a fragment of an old Tibetan song.

The land where spiritual and human law reign supreme,
In the land where celestial powers are revered,
Where animals are partners in life's struggle,
Where birds fly without fear,
Where fish swim in freedom,
Where wildlife is protected,
Where men and women cherish inner peace and outer freedom.

[1993]

The Wildlife Conservation Society

The Wildlife Conservation Society (formerly the New York Zoological Society) was established in 1895 as a nonprofit, tax-exempt organization to manage New York's zoos. However, WCS since its inception has also been concerned with the conservation of wildlife and habitats. Its first expedition went to Alaska in 1897 to survey the status of large mammals, and currently it is conducting more than three hundred field projects in about fifty nations.

The goal of WCS is to save wildlife and wildlands by understanding and resolving critical problems that threaten key species and large wild ecosystems around the world. WCS does this through careful research, education, and collaboration with communities and local institutions. It has helped to establish, guide, and support more than 120 wildlife reserves, and has promoted conservation and management of critical ecosystems to achieve a measure of harmony between local communities and their natural environment.

More about the worldwide conservation programs of WCS can be found on the Internet at www.wcs.org or www.wcs.org/international. Queries about WCS programs or those of other conservation organizations can be sent to International Conservation, Wildlife Conservation Society, 2300 Southern Boulevard, Bronx, New York 10460, USA. George Schaller can be reached at asiaprogram@wcs.org when he is not in the field.

Selected Bibliography

The first group of references comprises all the books I have authored or coauthored, and which make more details of my studies in Asia and Africa available to those who seek them. An asterisk (*) denotes a scientific volume. The second list contains selected references, mostly popular books, on subjects described in the articles.

Books by George Schaller

The Mountain Gorilla. Chicago: University of Chicago Press, 1963.

The Year of the Gorilla. Chicago: University of Chicago Press, 1964.

The Deer and the Tiger: A Study of Wildlife in India. Chicago: University of Chicago Press, 1967.

The Tiger: Its Life in the Wild (children's book, with M. Selsam). New York: Harper and Row, 1969

The Serengeti Lion. Chicago: University of Chicago Press, 1972.

Serengeti: A Kingdom of Predators. New York: Knopf, 1972.

Golden Shadows, Flying Hooves. New York: Knopf, 1973. Reprinted 1983, University of Chicago Press.

Mountain Monarchs: Wild Sheep and Goats of the Himalaya. Chicago: University of Chicago Press, 1977.

Wonders of Lions (children's book, with K. Schaller). New York: Dodd, Mead, 1977.

Stones of Silence: Journeys in the Himalaya. New York: Viking Press, 1980. Reprinted 1988, University of Chicago Press.

The Giant Pandas of Wolong (with J. Hu, W. Pan, and J. Zhu). Chicago: University of Chicago Press, 1985.

Gorilla: Struggle for Survival in the Virungas (with M. Nichols). New York: Aperture, 1989.

The Last Panda. Chicago: University of Chicago Press, 1993.

Tibet's Hidden Wilderness. New York: Harry N. Abrams, Inc., 1997.

Wildlife of the Tibetan Steppe. Chicago: University of Chicago Press, 1998.

Antelopes, Deer, and Relatives (E. Vrba and Schaller, eds.). New Haven, Conn.: Yale University Press, 2000.

SELECTED BIBLIOGRAPHY

Additional References

Banerjee, Subhankar. *Arctic National Wildlife Refuge: Seasons of Life and Land.* Seattle: The Mountaineers Books, 2003.

Bertram, Brian. *Pride of Lions.* London: J. M. Dent & Sons, 1978.

Campbell, Bob. *The Taming of the Gorillas.* London: Minerva Press, 2000.

Caro, Tim. *Cheetahs of the Serengeti Plains.* Chicago: University of Chicago Press, 1994.

Chavda, Divyabhanusinh. *The End of the Trail: The Cheetah in India.* New Delhi: Oxford University Press, 1999.

Fossey, Dian. *Gorillas in the Mist.* Boston: Houghton Mifflin Co., 1983.

Hillard, Darla. *Vanishing Tracks: Four Years among the Snow Leopards of Nepal.* New York: William Morrow, 1989.

Hunter, Luke, and Dave Hamman. *Cheetah.* Cape Town: Struik Publications, 2003.

Karanth, K. Ullas. *The Way of the Tiger.* Stillwater, Mont.: Voyageur Press, 2001.

Lindburg, Donald G., and Karen Baragona, eds. *Giant Pandas, Biology and Conservation.* Berkeley: University of California Press, 2004.

Lü, Zhi. *Giant Pandas in the Wild.* New York: Aperture, 2002.

Matthiessen, Peter. *The Snow Leopard.* New York: Viking Press, 1978.

Nichols, Michael, and Geoffrey Ward. *The Year of the Tiger.* Washington, D.C.: National Geographic Society, 1998.

Rabinowitz, Alan. *Jaguar: One Man's Struggle to Establish the World's First Jaguar Preserve.* New York: Arbor House, 1986.

Ridgeway, Rick. *The Big Open: On Foot across Tibet's Chang Tang.* Washington, D.C.: National Geographic Society, 2004.

Seidensticker, John, Sarah Christie, and Peter Jackson, eds. *Riding the Tiger: Tiger Conservation in Human-Dominated Landscapes.* Cambridge: Cambridge University Press, 1999.

Sunquist, Mel, and Fiona Sunquist. *Wild Cats of the World.* Chicago: University of Chicago Press, 2002.

Thapar, Valmik. *Tiger: The Ultimate Guide.* New York: CDS Books, 2004.

Waterman, Jonathan. *Where Mountains Are Nameless: Passion and Politics in the Arctic National Wildlife Refuge.* New York: W. W. Norton, 2005.

Weber, Bill, and Amy Vedder. *In the Kingdom of Gorillas: Fragile Species in a Dangerous Land.* New York: Simon and Schuster, 2001.

Credits for Reprinted Material

About the Author

George Schaller is a field biologist and vice president of the Wildlife Conservation Society in New York. Born in 1933, he did undergraduate work at the University of Alaska and graduate work at the University of Wisconsin. He has spent most of his career in the field in Asia, Africa, and South America, studying and working to protect wild creatures as diverse as the mountain gorilla, jaguar, panda, tiger, lion, and the wild sheep and goats of the Himalaya. These travels and studies have been the basis for his scientific and popular writings, which include acclaimed volumes such as *The Year of the Gorilla*, *The Serengeti Lion*, *The Last Panda*, and *Tibet's Hidden Wilderness*. For nearly two decades, Schaller has worked on the Tibetan Plateau in collaboration with Chinese and Tibetan scientists studying wildlife such as the Tibetan antelope (chiru), wild yak, and snow leopard, and promoting efforts to help these animals survive. In recent years he has also conducted conservation projects in Laos, Myanmar, Mongolia, Iran, Tajikistan, and other countries. His awards include the International Cosmos Prize (Japan) and the Tyler Prize for Environmental Achievement (United States).